Michael Schlemmer

Pattern Recognition for Feature-based and Comparative Visualization

Michael Schlemmer

Pattern Recognition for Feature-based and Comparative Visualization

Moment Invariants for Pattern Recognition in Flows

Südwestdeutscher Verlag für Hochschulschriften

Impressum/Imprint (nur für Deutschland/only for Germany)
Bibliografische Information der Deutschen Nationalbibliothek: Die Deutsche Nationalbibliothek verzeichnet diese Publikation in der Deutschen Nationalbibliografie; detaillierte bibliografische Daten sind im Internet über http://dnb.d-nb.de abrufbar.
Alle in diesem Buch genannten Marken und Produktnamen unterliegen warenzeichen-, marken- oder patentrechtlichem Schutz bzw. sind Warenzeichen oder eingetragene Warenzeichen der jeweiligen Inhaber. Die Wiedergabe von Marken, Produktnamen, Gebrauchsnamen, Handelsnamen, Warenbezeichnungen u.s.w. in diesem Werk berechtigt auch ohne besondere Kennzeichnung nicht zu der Annahme, dass solche Namen im Sinne der Warenzeichen- und Markenschutzgesetzgebung als frei zu betrachten wären und daher von jedermann benutzt werden dürften.

Coverbild: www.ingimage.com

Verlag: Südwestdeutscher Verlag für Hochschulschriften GmbH & Co. KG
Dudweiler Landstr. 99, 66123 Saarbrücken, Deutschland
Telefon +49 681 37 20 271-1, Telefax +49 681 37 20 271-0
Email: info@svh-verlag.de

Approved by: Kaiserslautern, TU, Auszug aus Diss., 2011

Herstellung in Deutschland:
Schaltungsdienst Lange o.H.G., Berlin
Books on Demand GmbH, Norderstedt
Reha GmbH, Saarbrücken
Amazon Distribution GmbH, Leipzig
ISBN: 978-3-8381-2757-6

Imprint (only for USA, GB)
Bibliographic information published by the Deutsche Nationalbibliothek: The Deutsche Nationalbibliothek lists this publication in the Deutsche Nationalbibliografie; detailed bibliographic data are available in the Internet at http://dnb.d-nb.de.
Any brand names and product names mentioned in this book are subject to trademark, brand or patent protection and are trademarks or registered trademarks of their respective holders. The use of brand names, product names, common names, trade names, product descriptions etc. even without a particular marking in this works is in no way to be construed to mean that such names may be regarded as unrestricted in respect of trademark and brand protection legislation and could thus be used by anyone.

Cover image: www.ingimage.com

Publisher: Südwestdeutscher Verlag für Hochschulschriften GmbH & Co. KG
Dudweiler Landstr. 99, 66123 Saarbrücken, Germany
Phone +49 681 37 20 271-1, Fax +49 681 37 20 271-0
Email: info@svh-verlag.de

Printed in the U.S.A.
Printed in the U.K. by (see last page)
ISBN: 978-3-8381-2757-6

Copyright © 2011 by the author and Südwestdeutscher Verlag für Hochschulschriften GmbH & Co. KG and licensors
All rights reserved. Saarbrücken 2011

For Benjamin and Sylvia.

Abstract

The recognition of patterns and structures has gained importance for dealing with the growing amount of data being generated by sensors and simulations. Most existing methods for pattern recognition are taylored for scalar data and non-correlated data of higher dimensions. The recognition of general patterns in flow structures (correlated data) is possible, but not yet practically usable, due to the high computatation effort. The main goal of this work is to present methods for *comparative visualization* of flow data, amongst others, based on a new method for efficient pattern recognition on flow data. This work is structured in three parts:

At first, a known feature-based approach for pattern recognition on flow data, the *Clifford convolution*, has been applied to color edge detection. However, this method is still computationally expensive for a general pattern recognition, since the recognition algorithm has to be applied for numerous different scales and orientations of the query pattern.

A more efficient and accurate method for pattern recognition on flow data is presented in the second part of this dissertation. It is based upon a novel mathematical formulation of *moment invariants for flow data*. The common *moment invariants* for *pattern recognition* are not applicable on flow data, since they are only invariant on non-correlated data. Because of the spatial correlation of flow data, the moment invariants had to be redefined with different basis functions to satisfy the demands for an invariant mapping of flow data. The computation of the moment invariants is done by a multi-scale convolution of the complete flow field with the basis functions. This pre-processing computation time almost equals the time for the pattern recognition of one single general pattern with the former algorithms. However, after having computed the moments once, they can be indexed and used as a look-up-table to recognize any desired pattern quickly and interactively (for data of common size). This results in a flexible and easy-to-use tool for the analysis of patterns in 2d flow data.

For an improved rendering of the recognized features, an importance driven streamline algorithm has been developed. The density of the streamlines can be adjusted by using importance maps. The result of a pattern recognition can be used as such a map, for example. Finally, new comparative flow visualization approaches utilizing the streamline approach, the flow pattern matching, and the moment invariants are presented.

Contents

1 **Introduction**   1
    1.1   Context and Goals 1
    1.2   Related Concepts 2
    1.3   Proposed Concepts 5

I   Foundations and State of the Art   8

2 **Foundations**   9
    2.1   Flow Visualization (Basics and Overview) 11
        2.1.1   Feature Based Visualization 12
        2.1.2   Basics of Clifford algebra 14
        2.1.3   Streamline Techniques 16
        2.1.4   Comparative Flow Visualization 18
    2.2   Basics of Image Processing 20
        2.2.1   Correlation and Convolution 21
        2.2.2   Fourier Transform 24
            2.2.2.1   Definition and Properties 24
            2.2.2.2   Fast Fourier Transform (FFT) 28
    2.3   Moment Invariants for Scalar Data 28
        2.3.1   Moments 29
        2.3.2   Translation Invariance 30
        2.3.3   Scale Invariance 33
        2.3.4   Rotation Invariance 34

        2.3.5   Construction of an Invariant Moment Basis 38

3 **State of the Art: Image Processing for Flow Visualization**   **41**
   3.1 Clifford Convolution 41
   3.2 Pattern Matching on Vector Fields 44
   3.3 Clifford FFT 47
   3.4 Open Questions 51

II Extension of the Clifford-based Approach   53

4 **Color Edge Detection using Clifford Algebra**   **54**
   4.1 Gray-scale Edge Detection 54
   4.2 Color Edge Detection Approaches 56
   4.3 Clifford Color Edge Detection 57
        4.3.1   Data Structure 57
        4.3.2   Choice of patterns 58
        4.3.3   The Detection Algorithm 59
        4.3.4   Application Results 61
   4.4 Conclusions 63

III Flow Pattern Recognition using Moment Invariants 66

5 **Generalized Moment Invariants**   **67**
   5.1 Definition of Moment Invariants for Flow Data 68
        5.1.1   Moments for Flows 69
        5.1.2   Translation Invariance 70
        5.1.3   Scale Invariance 73
                5.1.3.1   Domain Scale Invariance 73
                5.1.3.2   Total Scale Invariance 76
        5.1.4   Complex Flow Moments 78
        5.1.5   Rotation Invariance 79
        5.1.6   Construction of an Invariant Moment Basis for Flows 81

Contents iii

    5.2   Critical Point Characteristics of Flow Moments 89

6 Algorithms for Fast Flow Pattern Recognition   94
    6.1   Moment Pyramid 95
           6.1.1   Correlation with Moment Filter Masks 96
           6.1.2   Overcoming Discretization Issues 97
           6.1.3   Multi-scale Moment Pyramid 98
           6.1.4   Generalization 98
    6.2   Critical point recognition and visualization 100
    6.3   Fast Pattern Recognition in Flow Fields 101

IV Context-based and Comparative Flow Visualization 108

7 Priority Streamlines   109
    7.1   Definition of the Streamline Density 110
    7.2   Priority Streamline Algorithm 113
           7.2.1   General Idea 113
           7.2.2   Density Map 114
           7.2.3   Streamline Seeding 114
           7.2.4   Calculation of the Streamlines 115
    7.3   Construction of the Density Map 117
    7.4   Filtering 118
    7.5   Results 121
    7.6   Conclusions 123

8 Comparative Visualization   125
    8.1   Comparative Streamline Visualization 125
    8.2   Interactive Pattern Comparison 130
    8.3   Comparative Visualization of Time-Variant Data 136
           8.3.1   Difference Metrics 136
           8.3.2   Interactive Pattern Comparison 137
           8.3.3   Moment Pyramid Comparison 139

9 Conclusions	**144**
References	**148**
List of Figures	**156**
A Data Description	**158**
A.1 Boussinesq Flow	158
A.2 Hurricane Isabel	158
A.3 Mantle Convection Data	158
A.4 Mixing Layer	159
A.5 Swirling Jet Data	159
Publications	**161**

Chapter 1

Introduction

1.1 Context and Goals

The analysis of flow features is of great importance in many application areas. Weather forecasts are for example based on analyses of air and water flows. In *geology*, scientists are researching magma flows to forecast possible earthquakes or volcano eruptions. In industry, cars are designed to have a low specific fuel consumption. This can be achieved by a computer simulation or experimental analysis of the air flow around the car in a wind tunnel.

The analysis of flow features can be performed in multiple different and sophisticated ways. However, pure statistical analyses do not reveal a complete picture of the information contained in large amounts of data. With increasing amounts of data, the area of *flow visualization* becomes increasingly important.

In the context of *flow visualization* there has been really good progress over the last twenty years. Many sophisticated methods have been developed for the proper visualization of flow. However, the comparison of flows is by far not as investigated as the analyses and visualization methods for single flow fields. In application areas like *meteorology* it can be important to compare different weather situations, e.g., a comparison of the current air flow with flows at the time of the development of a hurricane. *Comparative visualization* of flow data is yet mainly limited to a side-by-side image comparison. So, the main goal of this work is to contribute an alternative concept for *comparative visualization* using *pattern recognition* on *flow data*.

To develop this concept, methods from the area of *image processing* and *computer vision* (ACM: I.4) and *pattern recognition* (ACM: I.5) have been adapted and refined for application in the area of *visualization* (ACM: I.3 *computer graphics*), according to the ACM classifications [Jon98].

The main idea of this work is to provide an efficient, robust, and accurate method enabling a fast comparision of 2d flow patterns. For this reason, *moment invariants*, a technique from *computer vision* have been adapted and revised for this purpose. The revision of *moment invariants* to flow data is the major theoretical contribution of this work, since the adaptation was not a simple component-wise application of the same functions. A complete revision of the basis functions was necessary to achieve the goal.

This main part is concentrating strongly on the filtering process in context of the visualization pipeline. Besides the development of new filtering techniques for flow and image data, this work is also tackling the rendering part of the pipeline, by the development of an importance driven streamline visualization, offering an alternative approach for *comparative visualization* of flows in 2d and 3d.

1.2 Related Concepts

Flow visualization can be achieved in various ways, since flow data can be analyzed from different points of view. Most of the flow visualization methods focus on the topological behavior of flows. A major part of the description of a flow topology are critical points of the flow, i.e. rotations, swirls, sinks, sources, and saddles for two dimensional flows. Streamlines integrated from saddles (*separatrices*) are used to distinguish between different flow regions. Besides this topological visualization approach, there is the so-called *feature based visualization*. This class of visualization methods is dedicated to highlight certain features of a flow field. Most of the

1.2 Related Concepts 3

known feature based approaches focus on the mentioned *topological features*. For more details on these methods see chapter 2.

Comparative visualization can be regarded from several points of view. The term is often used for a side-by-side image comparison. A similar point of view is the visualization of a comparison by difference images. A different idea is the approach of comparing streamlines of flows. These methods will be reflected in chapter 2.1.4. It will be discussed, why they are not yet sufficient for the task of a usable comparative visualization. So far, there is no efficient way for a comparative visualization of flows, enabling an application researcher or engineer to really compare two or more flow data sets with the goal to find similar pattern structures.

The combination of the areas *computer vision* and *visualization* has already been applied in the context of *feature based flow visualization*. Mainly two of these methods are discussed in chapter 3. Their goal is to recognize a given flow pattern (further called *query pattern*) in a flow data set. They are both based on the correlation operator, a basic tool from *image processing*. Heiberg et al. [HEWK03] proposed the correlation using the scalar product for vectors. Ebling and Scheuermann [ES03] replaced this scalar product by the *Clifford product*, combining scalar and cross product. For these approaches, it can be observed that pattern matching can be performed efficiently for special features, being invariant to rotation and scaling. For general features, however, these methods are not efficient (and not accurate) enough. Since the process of comparing one (general) flow pattern with another data set takes several minutes (regardless from hardware issues), these approaches are not usable for comparative flow analyses, in practice. Both methods, their extensions, advantages and disadvantages are presented and discussed in-depth in chapter 3.

Besides the *visualization*, it is also important to mention some ideas from *image processing* that are incorporated in this dissertation.

Image processing is generally performed in five phases: image acquisition, digitalization of the image, feature extraction by filter application, segmentation (region identification), and classification. Having a digitalized image, an edge detection is performed, in general by a correlation with specific edge detection filter masks. Given the edges, regions are identified, for example by connected edges or by a Hough transform. This process is also called segmentation. Finally the regions are classified as certain objects.

While image acquisition and digitalization are not of importance in our context, the feature extraction and classification are very interesting for the purpose of visualization (especially for the filtering phase of the visualization pipeline). As mentioned, the feature extraction tools *correlation* and *convolution* have already been applied in the context of flow visualization. Since a general feature detection is the goal of this work, the classification is also of high interest. A possible method for classification of images is the application of *moment invariants*.

Moment invariants are a geometry based tool for the classification of image data. In other words, they are special mathematical feature vectors, being invariant to translation, scaling, and rotation. They are extremely useful, for example in character recognition. Images of characters obtain specific geometric characteristics. The *moment invariants* deliver a set of characteristic values for a certain character. Thus, by looking up known moment invariant values, the characters can be recognized. This is especially important for OCR (*optical character recognition*), applications being used for the digitization of documents .

Moment invariants are not limited to character classification. They can also be applied onto all other kinds of images. Generally, they are only applied on specific regions, previously extracted by a segmentation step.

Besides feature extraction techniques from *image processing*, *moment invariants* represent an essential tool for this dissertation. These basic foundations for this work will be discussed in detail in chapter 2.

1.3 Proposed Concepts

The first concept presented in this dissertation is an application of the *Clifford convolution* and *Clifford Fourier transform* for an improved recognition of edges in color images. Both, the *Clifford convolution* and *Clifford Fourier transform* are designed for handling vector data on uniform grids. Moreover, the *Clifford algebra* offers the opportunity to additionally handle complex scalar data in the data structure *multi-vector*. Color images can be represented using various color models. Computers normally use the RGB (**R**ed, **G**reen, **B**lue) color model, television screens are usually using YUV (Y ≡ luminance, UV ≡ chrominance) or related models. Those models are very similar and can be transformed into one another without loss by a simple linear operation. Using the YUV model, the color image can be described as a *Clifford multi-vector*, using the luminance as scalar and the chrominance as vector part. The recognition of 2D critical points of flow fields yields the recognition of edges in the chrominance part of the given color image. The results show that the recognition of edges in color images is improved, compared to a common gray-scale edge detection.

The main focus of the dissertation is an improved *pattern recognition* concept to utilize *feature based* and *comparative visualization*. This work presents a novel technique to enable interactive *pattern recognition* in flows for general query patterns. Yet existing methods are only capable of providing a fast recognition only for special features. For a general choice of the query pattern those methods are much too slow or too inaccurate to really provide a usable tool for application researchers and engineers. To solve this problem, a novel mathematical formulation of *moment invariants for flows* is introduced.

These *flow moment invariants* describe a flow pattern regardless of its position, scale, and its orientation. The main issues here are the scale and rotation invariance. There are different possibilities for defining these invariances, as for example in contrast to the scaling of an image, a flow vector pattern is not only scalable by the grid size, but also in terms of vector lengths.

The biggest difference between flow moments and image moments is that the rotation invariance has to be warranted differently. For the image case, there the orientation of a single element (pixel) is of no importance. Only the global orientation of the pattern is taken into account. In case of a flow field, however, the orientation of a single element contains essential information: the direction of the vector. A component-wise application of the image moments does not result in a proper description for flow patterns. Thus, the basis functions of the *moment invariants* are modified, to obtain a correct description of *moment invariants for flows*.

With the *flow moment invariants*, it is possible to classify flow patterns invariantly from scale and orientation. In *image processing*, classification is one of the final steps in a long chain of actions. So, *moment invariants* are in general applied to pre-segmented and pre-processed portions of scalar image data. In the context of this work, it is not possible to assume a pre-segmented portion of data, since a major goal is to recognize any given arbitrarily structured pattern. However, the application of a segmentation would introduce topological restrictions. Thus, in contrast to *image processing*, *moment invariants* have to be applied directly on the whole non-pre-segmented data, to obtain meaningful results.

Under these conditions it is possible to detect any given query pattern, or similar versions, in a given data set. This can be done for images, using the common scalar *moment invariants*, and for flow data, using the novel *flow moment invariants*. This *pattern recognition* for feature based visualization is presented in chapter 6. The actual *pattern recognition* can be performed interactively for commonly sized data sets, while other methods need several minutes for completing this task.

This novel interactive *pattern recognition* for scalar data and flows can be utilized to perform comparative visualization. One scenario is for example to compare patterns in one data set. The user selects a (flow) pattern by placing a region marker. Similar patterns are highlighted in the visualization of the data-set. Moving or resizing the region marker changes the query pattern. Since this can be done interactively, the user has a tool for finding similarities in a data set quickly. Extending this method to multiple data sets results in a complete comparative visualization environment.

1.3 Proposed Concepts

The region marker is used on one data set, while results are highlighted in all data sets. This is a novel pattern based comparative visualization method.

A second idea for comparative visualization is to observe differences between neighboring time steps of time-variant data. Subtracting two moment representation of neighboring data slices results in a pattern-based multi-scale comparison. This is somewhat similar to the computation of a Laplace pyramid. Besides performing this comparison locally for different scales, the local comparisons can be compiled into a global result, using different metrics for combination. The comparative visualization concepts are presented in chapter 8.

The results of a *pattern recognition* are in general scalar data fields, representing the similarities of the analyzed data set to special query patterns. Having several queries to be visualized in parallel, there is the problem to find a proper visualization, especially in flow visualization. For this reason, a visualization concept serving this need has been developed in the context of this work. The so called *priority streamlines*, presented in chapter 7, can draw streamlines with density according to a given scalar map. Using different colors for the streamlines, it is possible to offer a complete picture of the flow, as well as to highlight special regions by using a higher density of streamlines with the corresponding color. This visualization enables a user to observe many different query results in parallel. *Priority streamlines* can also be used to visualize and observe other scalar features of flow data, i.e. derived features like vorticity or velocity, as well as additionally given features like pressure, temperature, etc., also in three dimensions.

Finally, in chapter 9 the work is concluded, open questions and further alternatives to the presented *moment invariants* are discussed in detail.

Part I

Foundations and State of the Art

Chapter 2

Foundations

In this dissertation two areas of computer science are addressed at once. The main goal of this work is providing enhanced *flow visualization* methods. For this purpose ideas from *image processing* are utilized. Thus, there is a need to present some basic foundations, to give an overview of all for this work meaningful foundations. This part of the dissertation presents basic ideas, terms, and notations from *flow visualization* (section 2.1) and *image processing* (section 2.2) as far as needed. While the current chapter gives a brief overview of basic and closely related topics of both areas separately, the following chapter 3 is giving more detailed information on the State-of-the-Art in *pattern recognition for flow fields*.

In both discussed research fields, there is a descriptive process pipeline. In the following, simplified versions of the *visualization pipeline* and the *image processing pipeline* are compared with each other. The comparison yields a general data processing pipeline being a cut set of both methodologies. Figure 2.1 illustrates all three pipelines. The *image processing pipeline* is located on the left, the *visualization pipeline* is located on the right. The formulation of a generalized pipeline has been placed in the middle of both known pipelines. Three coarse phases can be distinguished: a *data acquisition and preparation* phase provides the *data* that needs to be processed. The processing is mainly done in a *filtering and classification* phase. The output of this phase is additional *information* being the basis for the following *application* phase. In case of *image processing* the application is open and depends strongly on the application area. However, in *visualization*, the final goal

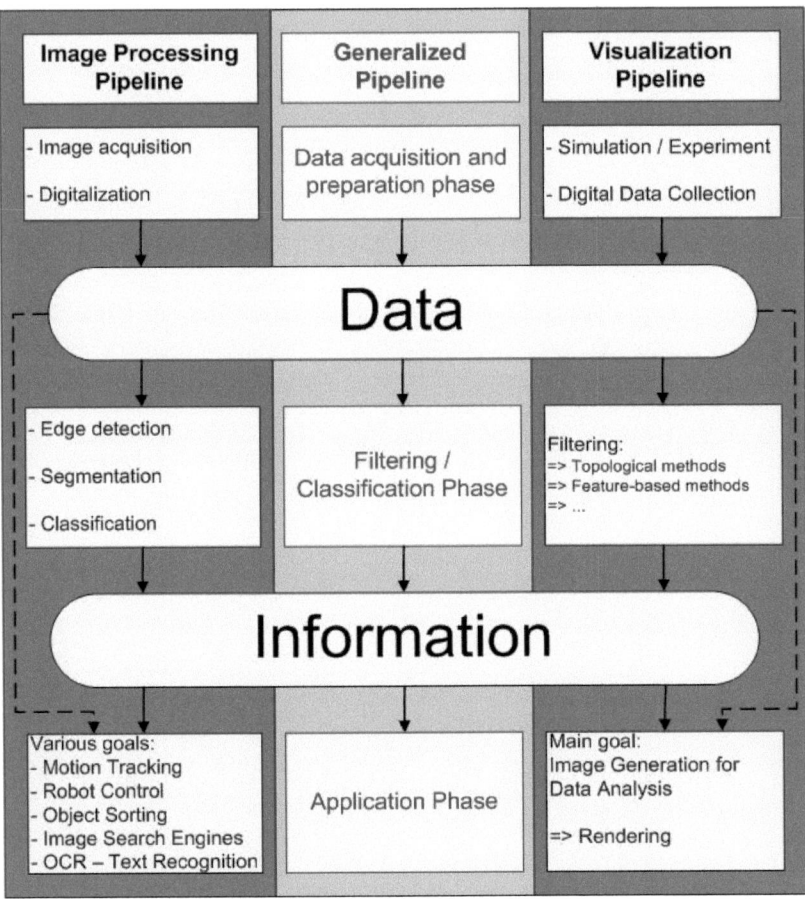

Figure 2.1: Generalized pipeline combined from simplified representations of the data processing pipelines from *visualization* and *image processing*.

is in general to provide a sophisticated visual representation of the data and its underlying phenomena. This dissertation is mainly dedicated to the *filtering process*, as illustrated in chapter 1.1.

In the area of *flow visualization* there are different types of approaches. We will concentrate on the two for this dissertation relevant methodologies, the *feature based* (see section 2.1.1) and the *comparative visualization* (see section 2.1.4). In the context of *feature based visualization* topological methods and some background information on *Clifford algebra* are included. Since *streamline techniques* are of importance for chapter 7 of this work, an extra section is added to discuss some basic ideas for their generation and improvement (section 2.1.3).

Some methods from the area of *image processing* (e.g. the *fast Fourier transform*, or the *convolution* operator) have already been adapted to flow data. In the context of this work, ideas of image processing and understanding play a very important role in the filtering process. So, section 2.2 is dedicated to *image processing* and *image classification* methods.

2.1 Flow Visualization (Basics and Overview)

An important area of *scientific visualization* is focusing on the visualization of flows. Flows are specific dynamical systems, thus, visualization of flows is strongly related to dynamical system visualization. While scientists and engineers formerly used smoke and dyes to visualize flow practically, flow visualization is nowadays mostly done on a computational basis. Fluid flows (e.g. water, fuel, magma) as well as gaseous flows (e.g. air, wind, natural gas) are simulated in the research field of *computational fluid dynamics* (*CFD*). Often, finite element methods are used to handle complex flow structures, e.g., local solvers of the Navier-Stokes equations, which work on various kinds of grids. *CFD* usually produces data sets providing huge amounts of sampled vector information on two- or three-dimensional domains.

The purpose of flow visualization is to facilitate investigation and analysis of the given flow structures. While direct flow visualization (e.g. hedgehogs, flow probes, textures) can give complete, but often cluttered visual representations, more sophisticated visualization methods reduce large amounts of data to the most important information. The major issue of these visualizations is to highlight essential facts hidden in the data. Of course, the main question is, *what is essential about the data and what is not?*

For flow visualization, this question is approached differently by various communities. The *topology based flow visualization* community is focusing on the *topology* of a flow field. *Feature based techniques* are often referring to topological information, focusing on a sophisticated representation and visualization of specific flow field characteristics. Streamline and stream surface techniques are valuable geometrical visualization tools, often being applied in this context. A rather immature area of visualization gaining more and more attention nowadays is the area of comparative visualization. The yet known methods are related to feature based techniques.

This section will give an overview over the mentioned areas of *flow visualization*. In context of *feature based visualization*, topological methods will also be discussed briefly. As *streamlines* are of special interest for this work, a section is dedicated to this topic. For more details the interested reader is referred to a good general overview of common flow visualization techniques that has been presented by Hauser et al. [HLD02]. Recently, Weiskopf and Erlebacher [WE04] published a more up to date overview in the *Visualization Handbook* [HJ04]. Finally, the area *comparative visualization* is outlined and discussed.

2.1.1 Feature Based Visualization

The *feature based visualization* approach is basically concerned with the visualization of interesting characteristics of flow data. There are several possibilities for defining these characteristics. One way to highlight features or characteristics is the extraction of physically meaningful patterns from the data. The definition of what is interesting, the way these features are extracted and the final visualization are dependent on the application, the data set, and the questions that scientists or

2.1 Flow Visualization (Basics and Overview)

engineers want to be clarified. Post et al. [PVH+02] presented a general overview over *feature based flow visualization*. This dissertation will, however, concentrate on certain details, being of interest for the research part of this work.

One possibility for the extraction of features is the observation of special topology patterns. Even though, the foundations of topological methods go back to the work of fluid dynamicists from the 1960s (e.g., Lighthill [Lig63]), or the theoretical framework by Poincaré [Poi75], topological methods for the visualization of vector data have first been proposed by Helman and Hesselink [HH89b, HH89a, HH90, HH91]. The main issue topological methods are interested in are critical points of vector fields. As critical points are also of interest in the further context of this work, formal definitions of a *steady vector field* and *critical points* are given:

Definition 2.1.1 (Steady Vector Field)
*Let G be a subset of $\mathbb{R}^n$. A **steady vector field** f is represented by a vector-valued function $f : G \to \mathbb{R}^n$ in Euclidean coordinates $(x_1, ..., x_n)$. Further (see [Asi93]), steady (time-independent) vector fields can be represented by an autonomous ordinary differential equation:*

$$\frac{dx}{dt} = f(x).$$

This dissertation is focusing on steady vector fields. For simplification, the general terminology *vector field* will in the following apply to steady vector fields unless not declared otherwise. Those vector fields are not changing their flow behavior over time. A time-dependent vector field can be understood as a sequence of steady vector fields [Asi93]. As in practice, data is given discretely, there is no need for a definition of time-dependent flow fields in this dissertation. The following pattern recognition algorithms are focusing on purely spatial patterns.

In chapter 4 the term *vector field* also applies to color images, representing special vector fields as compositions of two or three scalar fields. So, the vector fields representing flow data are further called *flow fields*. In particular, a flow field (even a steady one) is *not* just a collection of scalar fields.

The following definition of a *critical point* is formulated generally for all kinds of vector fields.

Definition 2.1.2 (Critical Point)
A ***critical point*** $\mathbf{x_0} \in G \subseteq \mathbb{R}^n$ *of a vector field* $f : G \to \mathbb{R}^n$ *is characterized by*

$$\mathbf{f(x_0) = 0}.$$

A topological skeleton of a vector field is given by the set of all critical points and all stable and unstable manifolds of saddle points. For saddle points in a 2D vector field these manifolds are special streamlines (see section 2.1.3) called *separatrices*. In 3D, the role of the saddle points is taken by the 3D saddles and the spiral saddles, as defined, e.g. in [Asi93]. Their stable and unstable manifolds come in a pair of a 1D and a 2D manifold. The 2D manifolds are special stream surfaces, providing a segmentation of the field, similarly to the streamlines in the 2D case. In context of a visualization of stream surfaces, there is the issue of occlusion. For this reason, methods for topology simplification have been introduced by de Leeuw and van Liere [dLvL99] as well as Tricoche et al. [TSH00]. Moreover, this issue can be overcome for example by visualizing not the stream surfaces themselves, but their intersection points, the so-called saddle connectors, as proposed by Theisel et al. [TWHS03].

Considering the use of vector field topology for visualizing flow field data from the CFD area, topological features are not necessarily the final result an engineer or scientist is interested in. However, a topological analysis can be a valuable first step to be followed by other visualization techniques.

An overview of work in this area was given by Levit in 1992 [Lev92].

2.1.2 Basics of Clifford algebra

A further approach for the topological analysis of flow fields has been proposed by Scheuermann [Sch99]. A major goal of his work was the *detection and analysis of higher order critical points [...] by an approach based on Clifford analysis* [Sch99].

2.1 Flow Visualization (Basics and Overview)

The *Clifford algebra* was developed by William K. Clifford [Cli78] in the 19th century. The algebra extends the vector space used in analytic geometry by a special vector multiplication. This *Clifford multiplication* has a geometric meaning, for example rotations of objects can be formulated very easy in terms of Clifford algebra. It has also been basis for current pattern matching algorithms for vector fields (chapter 3) that are going to be extended in this dissertation (chapters 5 and 6). Thus, some basic definitions from the work of Scheuermann [Sch99] describing the Clifford algebra in 2D are given in this section.

The 2D Clifford algebra can be understood as an extension of complex numbers to vectors:

Definition 2.1.3 *Let $\mathbb{E}^2$ be the $\mathbb{R}$ vector space with basis $\{e_1, e_2\}$. The **Clifford algebra** $\mathcal{G}^2$ is the real 2^2-vector space with basis*

$$\{1, e_1, e_2, e_1 e_2\},$$

where

1. *$1 e_k = e_k$, $k = 1, 2$,*

2. *$e_k e_k = 1$, $k = 1, 2$, and*

3. *$e_k e_l = -e_l e_k$, $k \neq l$.*

Further, i_2 is defined as $i_2 = e_1 e_2$.

It is that $i_2^2 = i^2 = -1$, so i_2 is the imaginary number of the 2D-Clifford algebra.

Using these definitions, a non-commutative *Hodge-duality* can be derived:

$$e_2 = e_1 e_1 e_2 = e_1 i_2 \quad e_1 = e_1 e_2 e_2 = i_2 e_2$$

$$e_2 = e_2 e_1 e_1 = -i_2 e_1 \quad e_1 = e_2 e_2 e_1 = -e_2 i_2$$

The elements of a Clifford algebra are called multi-vectors. For the 2D case, they are shown in the following table:

name	grade	dimension	basis elements
scalar	0	1	1
vector	1	2	e_1, e_2
bivector	2	1	$e_1 e_2$

A multi-vector consists of a scalar, a 2D vector and the so-called bivector (pseudo-scalar). Regarding the Clifford algebra as an extension of complex numbers, it can be regarded as a tuple of two complex numbers, one having the scalar as real part and the bivector as imaginary part, the vector having the e_1 component as real and the e_2 component as imaginary part. For detailed information on Clifford algebra, see Hestenes and Sobczyk [HS99] or Lounesto [Lou01].

2.1.3 Streamline Techniques

The current section will give an overview over related streamline techniques. Prior to computer-driven visualization engineers used dyes in water or smoke in air for visualizing flows. Nowadays, computer simulation and analysis has gained much more importance. Thus, computers are also providing visual representations, for example geometric lines. *Streamlines* are commonly used for visualizing flow vector data. However, they are not the only geometric line representation of a flow field. There are different kinds of *flowlines*. According to Ward, they are defined as follows:

- ***Streaklines***: *simultaneous positions of a set of particles continuously released from one or more locations.*

- ***Pathlines***: *position at an instant of time of a batch of particles which had been released simultaneously.*

- ***Streamline***: *a line through the velocity field which is tangent to the velocity field at every point.*

For steady flow, streaklines, pathlines, and streamlines coincide. [War97]

This work will concentrate on steady flow and therefore only *streamlines*.

2.1 Flow Visualization (Basics and Overview)

Streamlines can be mathematically described, so today they are mostly numerically computed and visualized on computers. The formal definition of a streamline is done according to Garth [Gar07].

Definition 2.1.4 (Streamline)
*Let $G \subseteq \mathbb{R}^n$ and $f : G \to \mathbb{R}^n$ a vector field. A **streamline** $S(t,x)$ is an integral curve through in the dynamical system (flow) ϕ generated by f.*

In practice, streamlines are represented by polygon line strips. For a good visual representation the node points have to be chosen appropriately. These node points can be computed by solving the ordinary differential equation (ODE) representing the vector field (see definition 2.1.1). This can be done using numerical methods, i.e. the Eulerian method or the Runge-Kutta solver. More information on this topic can for example be found in a book of Butcher [But03] or alternatively in lecture notes from Heinrich [Hei00].

Streamlines for flow vector fields should, according to Verma et al. [VKP00], obey three basic issues:

- *Coverage:*
  No important flow feature should be missed. Flow features can be topological features as described by Verma et al. [VKP00]. In fact, flow features can also be defined more generally. We regard flow features as special patterns or regions being of (high) interest to the user.

- *Uniformity:*
  This principle argues that streamlines should be distributed more or less uniformly in the final image for better visual interpretation. This is of course a desirable criterion, especially for two dimensions. For 3D fields, one encounters severe problems when adhering to this principle. Each viewing direction results in a different density distribution in the final 2D projection. This could be overcome by a reduction of clutter or a 3D viewing device. Since we focus on the visualization of 3D data on computer screens, the criterion of uniformity is less important to reach our goal.

- *Continuity:*
  Another goal is to achieve an impression of continuity. This can be done by drawing long streamlines.

Because streamline seeding has a major influence on the resulting image, many methods optimize streamline seeding. First, Turk and Banks [TB96] focused on the uniformity of streamlines for 2D data, by presenting an image-guided streamline placement method. Mao et al. [MHHI98] transferred this method to curvilinear grids. Jobard and Lefer [JL97] presented an improved method for drawing evenly spaced streamlines in 2D space. Verma et al. [VKP00] were interested in covering all topological features and proposed a method that places streamline seeds in special patterns according to the topological features for 2D flows. Ye [YKP05] recently extended this approach for 3D topological patterns. Mattausch et al. [MTHG03] used illuminated, evenly spaced streamlines with additional color mapping for visualizing 3D flow vector data. Another method for efficient streamline seeding for 2D fields, the "farthest-point streamline seeding," appropriate for optimizing continuity, was published by Mebarki et al. [MAD05].

While some of these techniques mainly focus on uniformity or continuity, other methods focus on an optimal representation of topological features of the vector field. However, there is no method yet for drawing streamlines based on a user-defined context. This dissertation will present a context-based streamline method in chapter 7.

2.1.4 Comparative Flow Visualization

The area of *comparative visualization* has not yet been defined clearly. There are, to the author's knowledge, few publications on this topic regarding flow fields. Previous work on comparative visualization for flow fields includes the work of Pagendarm et al. [PW95]. In their terms, comparative visualization reduces to a simple side-by-side comparison of different data, rendered with the same method. However, this might result in wrong conclusions, as the visualization method itself takes a strong influence on the comparability.

2.1 Flow Visualization (Basics and Overview)

For this reason Verma and Pang [VP04] focused on a meaningful comparison of stream and vortex lines. Even though their method is using adaptive streamline placement, their method is also a kind of *post-visualization comparison*, since the comparative analysis is done based on the streamlines. Recently, Svakhine et al. [SJEG05] and Callahan et al. [CFS+06] have presented systems that supports comparative visualization views.

So, the area of *comparative flow visualization* is currently focusing on making visualizations *comparable*. In this dissertation, this goal will be approached differently by putting emphasize on the data analysis, using novel filtering methods to create additional information for visualization.

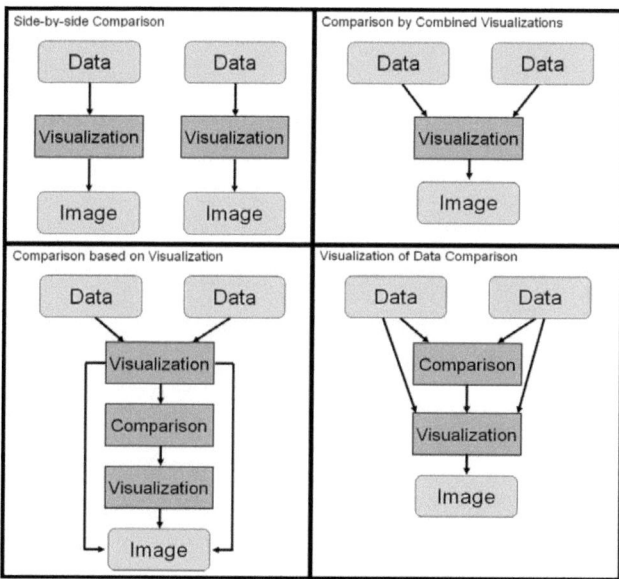

Figure 2.2: Four possible comparative visualization methods: side-by-side comparison, comparison by combined visualizations, comparison based on visualization, and visualization of data comparison.

This work defines *comparative visualization* by four different approaches for visual data comparison (see figure 2.2):

- *Side-by-side comparative visualization,*

- *comparison by combined visualization,*

- *comparison based on visualization,* and

- *visualization of data comparison.*

An advantage of the latter method is that the comparison is performed independent from the visualization, thus, being less error-prone. Of course, regarding the final visualization, there is the possibility of generating different hybrid variants of these basic methods. Chapter 8 will present enhanced side-by-side comparisons, as well as visualizations of a novel data comparison method.

2.2 Basics of Image Processing

Certain visualization approaches are utilizing *image processing* methods to generate visualizations. Thus, this section contains a brief introduction to some image processing methods, also being a basis for this work. The subject of *image processing* is the whole process from image acquisition and digitalization, to pattern recognition, and classification (see also figure 2.1). Applications of this area are widespread, e.g. OCE (text recognition) for generating ASCII text from scanned images, image search engines, robot control, structural testing and analysis of industrial parts, retinal scan evaluation for security purposes, computer tomography in medicine. The following sections 2.2.1 and 2.2.2 contain basic information on the pattern recognition process. section 2.3 gives a brief introduction to *moment invariants*, a geometrical classification method that is of fundamental interest for this dissertation.

2.2.1 Correlation and Convolution

The main purpose of image processing is the extraction of information from image data. Since *image processing* is mainly concerned with 2D images most definitions are formulated for the 2D case, but can be extended to any other dimensionality.

Definition 2.2.1 *A 2D-**image** is a discrete scalar function p over a uniform grid with N_1 grid points in direction x, N_2 grid points in direction y, with distances $\Delta x, \Delta y$ and value set $\mathbb{W} \subseteq \mathbb{C}$:*

$$p : \{0, 1\Delta x, ..., (N_1 - 1)\Delta x\} \times \{0, 1\Delta y, ..., (N_2 - 1)\Delta y\} \to \mathbb{W}.$$

*The discrete elements p_{ij} of the image are called **pixels** (picture elements):*

$$p_{ij} := p\left(\begin{pmatrix} i\Delta x \\ j\Delta y \end{pmatrix}\right)$$

A 2D-image is fully characterized by $P = (N_1, N_2, \Delta x, \Delta y, \mathbb{W}, \{p_{ij}\})$.

For 3D-images the discrete elements p_{ijk} are called *voxels* (volume elements).

For the analysis of images so-called *filter operations* can be defined. Filters are neighborhood-operations that are applied to images, for example to smoothen the image or to extract object edges.

Definition 2.2.2 *A **filter** of dimension d is defined as function*

$$F : \mathbb{W}^{N_1 \times ... \times N_d} \to \mathbb{W}^{N_1 \times ... \times N_d} \qquad (\mathbb{W} = \mathbb{R}, \mathbb{C})$$

mapping one image to another image.

Definition 2.2.3 *: A filter F of dimension d is called **linear**, if for any $p_1, p_2 \in \mathbb{W}^{N_1 \times ... \times N_d}, \alpha, \beta \in \mathbb{W}$:*

$$F(\alpha p_1 + \beta p_2) = \alpha F(p_1) + \beta F(p_2).$$

Definition 2.2.4 *Let S be a linear shift. A filter F is **shift-invariant**, if $S(F(p)) = F(S(p))$.*

Definition 2.2.5 : *A linear and shift-invariant filter is called **LSI-filter**.*

A LSI-filter can be fully described by its impulse response. A proof for this fact can be found in [Jäh95]. The application of a filter is performed using one of the operations *correlation* or *convolution*.

Definition 2.2.6 : *Let $g : \mathbb{R}^d \to \mathbb{C}$ be a signal and $h : \mathbb{R}^d \to \mathbb{C}$ a filter. The continuous **convolution** of the signal and the filter is defined by*

$$(g * h)(x) = \int_{\mathbb{R}^d} h(y)g(x-y)dy.$$

For discrete 2D-images a discrete convolution is formulated as follows:

Definition 2.2.7 *Let $M_d \leq N_d$ for $d = 1, 2$, let $g : \mathbb{W}^{N_1 \times N_2}$ be a 2D image and $h : \mathbb{W}^{M_1 \times M_2}$ be a filter. The **discrete convolution** of the image with the filter is defined as follows:*

$$(g * h)_{m,n} = \sum_{i=0}^{N_1-1} \sum_{j=0}^{N_2-1} h_{i,j} g_{m-i,n-j}.$$

The convolution process is illustrated in figure 2.3.

For recognition of image patterns one can perform a *correlation*. A correlation is equal to a convolution with a mirrored filter mask:

Definition 2.2.8 : *Let $g : \mathbb{R}^d \to \mathbb{C}$ be a signal and $h : \mathbb{R}^d \to \mathbb{C}$ be a filter. The continuous **correlation** of the signal and the filter is defined by*

$$(g \star h)(x) = \int_{\mathbb{R}^d} h(y)g(x+y)dy.$$

Definition 2.2.9 *Let $M_d \leq N_d$ for $d = 1, 2$, let $g : \mathbb{W}^{N_1 \times N_2}$ be a 2D image and $h : \mathbb{W}^{M_1 \times M_2}$ be a filter. The **discrete correlation** of the image with the filter is defined as follows:*

$$(g \star h)_{m,n} = \sum_{i=0}^{N_1-1} \sum_{j=0}^{N_2-1} h_{i,j} g_{m+i,n+j}.$$

2.2 Basics of Image Processing

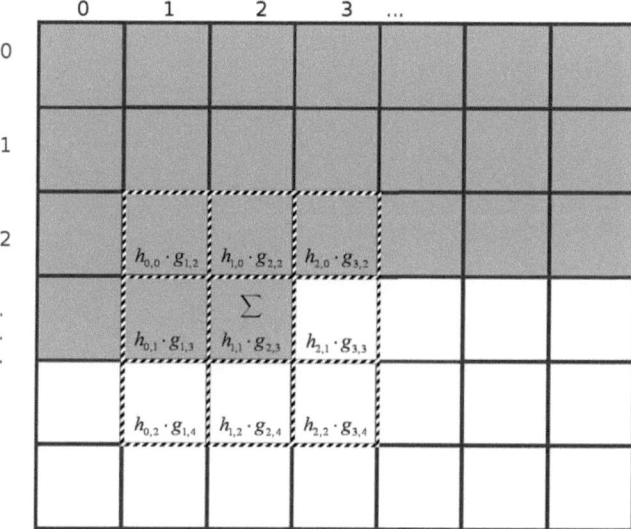

Figure 2.3: Illustration of the filtering process. The filter is traveling across the image. Each pixel value is multiplied and summed up. The result is written into a new filtered image at the current filter position. Moving the filter all over the original image results in a completely filtered image.

The *correlation* operation is very important, due to the fact that its application yields a *similarity image*, a comparison of an image with patterns, being defined by the filter. So, *correlation* enables computer driven *pattern matching* in image data. The role and importance of the *convolution* operator in this context will be clarified in section 2.2.2.

The computational complexity of the convolution and the correlation operation are in $O(n^2)$. It is possible to enhance this process by the use of a *fast Fourier transform (FFT)* (section 2.2.2).

Another issue is the treatment of the boundary values of the image. There are different possibilities, how the filtering can be performed at the boundaries:

- Fill missing boundary values with zeros.
- Extrapolate the missing boundary values.
- Use cyclic convolution, i.e. periodic boundary conditions.

None of these approaches is perfect, so Jähne advises not to depend on the boundary values and concentrate on the analysis of the inner data [Jäh95].

2.2.2 Fourier Transform

The *Fourier transform* is besides *correlation* and *convolution* one of the most important operations in *image processing*. A *Fourier transform* is a way to generate a frequency representation of data given in time and/or spatial domain. In case of *image processing*, the discrete 2D and 3D Fourier transforms are of high interest.

2.2.2.1 Definition and Properties

The Fourier transform is mathematically a change of the basis of the image. While in spatial domain, the basis is arranged pixel-wise (each basis image contains one grid point valued 1, all other points are 0) the Fourier representation builds up a completely different basis, spanned by (odd) sine functions and (even) cosine functions, or their representations in the complex Eulerian function space, respectively.

2.2 Basics of Image Processing

Definition 2.2.10 : Let $f : \mathbb{R}^k \to \mathbb{C}$ be a square integrable function. Then, the **continuous Fourier transform** is defined as follows:

$$\mathcal{F}_c\{f\}(u) = \hat{f}(u) = \int_{\mathbb{R}^k} f(x) e^{(-2\pi i u^T x)} d^k x.$$

The inverse continuous Fourier transform is for a square integrable function $\hat{f}(u) : \mathbb{R}^k \to \mathbb{C}$ defined by:

$$\mathcal{F}_c^{-1}\{\hat{f}\}(x) = f(x) = \int_{\mathbb{R}^k} \hat{f}(u) e^{(2\pi i u^T x)} d^k u$$

with $i^2 = -1$.

Writing $f(x) \circ\!\!\!-\!\!\!\bullet \hat{f}(u)$ means that $\hat{f}$ is the Fourier transformed of f.

As mentioned, in *image processing* discrete versions of the Fourier transform are of importance.

Definition 2.2.11 : The *1D-**discrete Fourier transform** (DFT)* is a map from a set of complex numbers g_n to another set of complex numbers $\hat{g}_v$:

$$\mathcal{DFT}\{g\} = \hat{g}_v = \frac{1}{\sqrt{N}} \sum_{n=0}^{N-1} g_n e^{-\frac{2\pi i n v}{N}}, \quad 0 \leq v \leq N.$$

The *2D-**discrete Fourier transform** (DFT)* is defined analogously:

$$\mathcal{DFT}\{g\} = \hat{g}_{v_1,v_2} = \frac{1}{\sqrt{N_1 N_2}} \sum_{n_1=0}^{N_1-1} \sum_{n_2=0}^{N_2-1} g_{n_1,n_2} e^{-\frac{2\pi i n_1 v_1}{N_1}} e^{-\frac{2\pi i n_2 v_2}{N_2}}.$$

The **inverse discrete Fourier Transforms** are defined as

$$\mathcal{DFT}^{-1}\{\hat{g}\} = g_n = \frac{1}{\sqrt{N}} \sum_{v=0}^{N-1} \hat{g}_v e^{\frac{2\pi i n v}{N}}, \quad 0 \leq n \leq N$$

for 1D, and for 2D as:

$$\mathcal{DFT}\{g\} = \hat{g}_{v_1,v_2} = \frac{1}{\sqrt{N_1 N_2}} \sum_{n_1=0}^{N_1-1} \sum_{n_2=0}^{N_2-1} g_{n_1,n_2} e^{\frac{2\pi i n_1 v_1}{N_1}} e^{\frac{2\pi i n_2 v_2}{N_2}}.$$

This definition has been adapted from one of different possible definitions given by Jähne [Jäh95]. There is one major property that is of major interest to *image processing* and also for this dissertation. Thus, only this property, the *convolution theorem* will be briefly discussed. More properties and facts about the Fourier transform can be found in [Jäh95, Jai89].

Theorem 2.2.1 (Convolution)
Let the pairs $g \circ\!\!-\!\!\bullet \hat{g}$ and $h \circ\!\!-\!\!\bullet \hat{h}$ be functions and their Fourier transformed. Then it is

...for the continuous case: $(g(x) * h(x)) \circ\!\!-\!\!\bullet (\hat{g}(u) \cdot \hat{h}(u))$
...for the 1D-DFT: $(g * h) \circ\!\!-\!\!\bullet N(\hat{g} \cdot \hat{h})$
...for the 2D-DFT: $(g * h) \circ\!\!-\!\!\bullet N_1 N_2 (\hat{g} \cdot \hat{h})$.

This theorem has been taken from [Sch04], where a valid proof can also be found.

Theorem 2.2.2 *A d-dimensional DFT can be formulated recursively by d one-dimensional Fourier transforms.*

Proof:

$$\mathcal{DFT}\{g\} = \hat{g}_{v_1,\ldots,v_d} = \frac{1}{\sqrt{N_1 \ldots N_d}} \sum_{n_1=0}^{N_1-1} \ldots \sum_{n_d=0}^{N_d-1} g_{n_1,\ldots,n_d} e^{\frac{-2\pi i n_1 v_1}{N_1}} \ldots e^{\frac{-2\pi i n_d v_d}{N_d}}$$

$$= \frac{1}{\sqrt{N_1}} \sum_{n_1=0}^{N_1-1} \left[\ldots \left[\frac{1}{\sqrt{N_{d-1}}} \sum_{n_{d-1}=0}^{N_{d-1}-1} \left(\frac{1}{\sqrt{N_d}} \sum_{n_d=0}^{N_d-1} g_{n_1,\ldots,n_d} e^{\frac{-2\pi i n_d v_d}{N_d}} \right) e^{\frac{-2\pi i n_{d-1} v_{d-1}}{N_{d-1}}} \right] \ldots \right] e^{\frac{-2\pi i n_1 v_1}{N_1}}$$

$$= \frac{1}{\sqrt{N_1}} \sum_{n_1=0}^{N_1-1} \left[\ldots \left[\frac{1}{\sqrt{N_{d-1}}} \sum_{n_{d-1}=0}^{N_{d-1}-1} \tilde{g}_{n_1,\ldots,n_{d-1},v_d} e^{\frac{-2\pi i n_{d-1} v_{d-1}}{N_{d-1}}} \right] \ldots \right] e^{\frac{-2\pi i n_1 v_1}{N_1}}$$

with

$$\tilde{g}_{n_1,\ldots,n_{d-1},v_d} = \mathcal{DFT}(g_{n_1,\ldots,n_d}) = \frac{1}{\sqrt{N_d}} \sum_{n_d=0}^{N_d-1} g_{n_1,\ldots,n_d} e^{\frac{-2\pi i n_d v_d}{N_d}}.$$

2.2 Basics of Image Processing

This process can be repeated in total d times. It yields:

$$\mathcal{DFT}\{g\} = \hat{g}_{v_1,\ldots,v_d} = \mathcal{DFT}\left(\mathcal{DFT}\left(\ldots\mathcal{DFT}(g_{n_1,\ldots,n_d})\ldots\right)\right).$$

□

Together with the fact that there is a fast calculation for the Fourier transform, the presented theorem 2.2.1 yields that convolutions and thus also correlations (convolutions of the mirrored signal) can be performed at much higher speed. This is, because the convolution can be performed as a multiplication in frequency domain that can be done with a complexity of $O(n)$. This is much faster compared to the convolution/correlation in spatial domain with $O(n^2)$. Of course, the Fourier transform also has to be taken into account. Hence, there is a way for a fast calculation.

2.2.2.2 Fast Fourier Transform (FFT)

Because of theorem 2.2.2, it is enough to describe a 1D-FFT. Cooley and Tukey [CT65] have invented a fast algorithm the *fast Fourier transform (FFT)* with a complexity of $O\left(n \ log_2(n)\right)$. It is assuming the grid size of the data to be $N_1 \times ... \times N_d$, with $N_i = 2^k, k \in \mathbb{N}$ for all $i \in \{1,...,d\}$. The reason for this is that the algorithm is splitting up the data into two parts in each step:

$$\begin{aligned}
\mathcal{DFT}\{g\} &= \sum_{n=0}^{N-1} g_n e^{-\frac{2\pi i n v}{N}} \\
&= \sum_{n=0}^{N/2-1} g_{2n} e^{-\frac{2\pi i 2 n v}{N}} + \sum_{n=0}^{N/2-1} g_{2n+1} e^{-\frac{2\pi i (2n+1) v}{N}} \\
&= \sum_{n=0}^{N/2-1} g_{2n} e^{-\frac{2\pi i n v}{N/2}} + e^{-\frac{2\pi i v}{N}} \sum_{n=0}^{N/2-1} g_{2n+1} e^{-\frac{2\pi i n v}{N/2}}.
\end{aligned}$$

This can be repeated until the denominator of the exponent has value 1. In this case, the sums have only one entity each. The exponent $e^{-\frac{2\pi i n v}{1}} = e^0 = 1$ can be reduced to 1 because $n = 0$. This means, the inner sums reduce to a pure coefficient each. There are only coefficients and *phase shifts* $\left(e^{-\frac{2\pi i v}{N}}\right)$ left. Since there are only shifts to consider, the actual Fourier transform can be calculated by a reverse bit order sorting of the coefficients. More information on the original FFT-algorithm can be found in [CT65]. Further information on related fast algorithms can be found in the books of Blahut [Bla85] as well as Besslich and Lu [BL90]. A very good library for performing FFT computations of any kind is the *FFTW* library by Frigo and Johnson [FJ97, FJ07]. There are also approaches for performing FFTs on non-uniformly spaced data. There are approaches for *NFFTs* for scalar data, for example by Fourmont [Fou03], and Kunis and Potts [KP07].

2.3 Moment Invariants for Scalar Data

Another aspect of the *image processing* area that plays an important role in the context of this work is the theory of *moment invariants*. *Moments* are a statistical measure being applied to images to analyze their geometric features. This is com-

2.3 Moment Invariants for Scalar Data

monly an early part of the *classification* process.

This section will present an in-depth overview of the *moment invariants* for scalar image data that is later on generalized to vector data. The chosen definitions, theorems and proofs are almost identical to the definitions of Flusser's [Flu00] complex scalar moment invariants. Originally, *moment invariants* have been presented by Hu [Hu62] in the early 1960s. His version was proven to be redundant and incomplete by Flusser [Flu00]. The independent and complete set of *moment invariants* is in the author's opinion a valid basis for the later transfer to flow data.

2.3.1 Moments

Moments can be defined for scalar valued maps $f : G \to \mathbb{R}$ given on an arbitrary dimensional domain $G \subseteq \mathbb{R}^d$, $d \in \mathbb{N}$:

Definition 2.3.1 (*Moment of order* $(p_1 + ... + p_d)$ *of a d-dimensional scalar field*) Let $f = f(x_1, ..., x_d)$, $f : G \to \mathbb{R}$ be a map over $G \subseteq \mathbb{R}^d$, $d \in \mathbb{N}$. Let further $p_1, ..., p_d \in \mathbb{N}$. A **moment** of order $(p_1 + ... + p_d)$ of f is defined as

$$m_{p_1...p_d} = \int\limits_{-\infty}^{\infty} ... \int\limits_{-\infty}^{\infty} x_1^{p_1}...x_d^{p_d} f(x_1, ..., x_d) dx_1...dx_d.$$

The final moment invariants presented in this work will be based upon complex moments being especially tailored for two-dimensional data. For this reason it makes sense to give a concrete definition of the two-dimensional moment invariants.

Definition 2.3.2 *(Moments of order* $(p + q)$ *of a 2D scalar field)* Let $f = f(x, y)$, $f : G \to \mathbb{R}$ be a map over $G \subseteq \mathbb{R}^2$. Let further be $p, q \in \mathbb{N}$. **Moments** of order $(p + q)$ of f are defined as

$$m_{pq} = \int\limits_{-\infty}^{\infty} \int\limits_{-\infty}^{\infty} x^p y^q f(x, y) dx dy.$$

Kenney and Keeping [KK51] have proven that the moments represent a basis transformation of the underlying function f.

In the next sections it will be shown how those moments m_{pq} can be made invariant to translation, scaling, and rotation.

2.3.2 Translation Invariance

Though translation invariance will not be used in the pattern search algorithm presented in section 6, it is a vital part of the theory of moment invariants that needs to be discussed. For the generation of translation invariant moments one needs to modify the moments m_{pq}, as given in Definition 2.3.2, so that the resulting moments result in the same values for an original function f and a shifted version $\tilde{f}$ of f. The definition of m_{pq} reveals that the moments are depending on global coordinates x and y. Substitution of those global coordinates with suitable local coordinates yields automatically translation invariance. In the field of Computer Vision it is common to compute the gray-scale centroid of the given image f. Regarding arbitrary scalar functions, however, the choice of a centroid is more difficult, as for negative valued scalar fields the centroid is not always defined. For this reason, translation invariance is derived differently to the Computer Vision approach by utilization of the characteristic function χ_f of f.

Definition 2.3.3 (*Characteristic function of a scalar field*)
Let $f = f(x,y)$, $f : G \to \mathbb{R}$ be a map over $G \subseteq \mathbb{R}^2$. The characteristic function $\chi_f : G \to \{0,1\}$ of f is defined as

$$\chi_f(x,y) = \begin{cases} 1 & , \text{ if } f(x,y) \neq 0 \\ 0 & , \text{ if } f(x,y) = 0 \end{cases}.$$

The centroid of this characteristic function can be applied to obtain moments being invariant to translation, similarly to the centroid of f. Based upon this observation one can define the *central moments* and prove their invariance to a translation of the underlying function.

Definition 2.3.4 (*Central moments*)
Let $f = f(x,y)$, $f : G \to \mathbb{R}$ be a map over $G \subseteq \mathbb{R}^2$ and χ_f its corresponding characteristic function according to Definition 2.3.3. Let $p,q \in \mathbb{N}$ and let $m_{pq}^{\chi_f}$ be

2.3 Moment Invariants for Scalar Data

moments of the function χ_f. The **Central Moment** of order $(p+q)$ of f is defined as

$$\mu_{pq} = \int_{-\infty}^{\infty}\int_{-\infty}^{\infty} (x-\bar{x})^p(y-\bar{y})^q f(x,y)dxdy,$$

with

$$\bar{x} = \frac{m_{10}^{\chi_f}}{m_{00}^{\chi_f}} \quad \text{and} \quad \bar{y} = \frac{m_{01}^{\chi_f}}{m_{00}^{\chi_f}}$$

being the coordinates of the centroid of χ_f.

Theorem 2.3.1 (Invariance to translation)
Central Moments μ_{pq} of a map $f : G \to \mathbb{R}$, $G \subseteq \mathbb{R}^2$ are invariant to translations. This means their value is independent and therefore does not change for any translation of f by any vector $v = (v_1, v_2) \in \mathbb{R}^2$.

Proof: Let $\tilde{f}$ be a copy of f being translated with translation vector v: $\tilde{f}(x,y) = f(x-v_1, y-v_2)$. Then, $\tilde{\mu}_{pq}$ is the central moment of order $(p+q)$ of $\tilde{f}$. The centroid of $\chi_{\tilde{f}}$ is according to definition 2.3.4 defined as $(\bar{x}+v_1, \bar{y}+v_2)$. The statement can be proven by using the substitution $\lambda(x,y) = (x-v_1, y-v_2)^T$:

$$\mu_{pq} = \int_{-\infty}^{\infty}\int_{-\infty}^{\infty}(x-\bar{x})^p(y-\bar{y})^q f(x,y)dxdy$$

$$\stackrel{\lambda}{=} \int_{-\infty}^{\infty}\int_{-\infty}^{\infty}(x-v_1-\bar{x})^p(y-v_2-\bar{y})^q f(x-v_1, y-v_2)\left|\det\begin{pmatrix}1 & 0 \\ 0 & 1\end{pmatrix}\right| dxdy$$

$$= \int_{-\infty}^{\infty}\int_{-\infty}^{\infty}(x-(\bar{x}+v_1))^p(y-(\bar{y}+v_2))^q \tilde{f}(x,y)dxdy$$

$$= \tilde{\mu}_{pq}$$

□

The central moments μ_{pq} can be derived from the original moments m_{pq} by application of the binomial theorem:

$$\begin{aligned}
\mu_{pq} &= \int_{-\infty}^{\infty}\int_{-\infty}^{\infty} (x-\bar{x})^p (y-\bar{y})^q f(x,y) dx dy \\
&= \int_{-\infty}^{\infty}\int_{-\infty}^{\infty} \sum_{j=0}^{p} \binom{p}{j} x^j (-\bar{x})^{p-j} \sum_{k=0}^{q} \binom{q}{k} y^k (-\bar{y})^{q-k} f(x,y) dx dy \\
&= \sum_{j=0}^{p}\sum_{k=0}^{q} \binom{p}{j}\binom{q}{k} (-\bar{x})^{p-j}(-\bar{y})^{q-k} \int_{-\infty}^{\infty}\int_{-\infty}^{\infty} x^j y^k f(x,y) dx dy \\
&= \sum_{j=0}^{p}\sum_{k=0}^{q} \binom{p}{j}\binom{q}{k} (-\bar{x})^{p-j}(-\bar{y})^{q-k} m_{jk}
\end{aligned}$$

2.3.3 Scale Invariance

For a pattern recognition task it is very important recognizing similar structures at different scales. This can also be achieved by defining moments being invariant to scaling operations. For the derivation of scale invariant moments, m_{pq} as well as the translation invariant central moments μ_{pq} can be used as a basis. The derivation is shown for μ_{pq} though it can be substituted by m_{pq} in the following paragraph.

To obtain scale invariance the given moments have to be normalized according to a certain power of the volume of f or a proportional item, respectively. The volume of f is trivially given by m_{00} or equally μ_{00}. Thus, an order dependent power of the precalculated μ_{00} can be used for scale normalization of the moments μ_{pq}. In the following the so called normalized central moments are defined and their scale invariance is shown.

Definition 2.3.5 *(Normalized Central Moments)*
Let $f = f(x,y)$, $f : G \to \mathbb{R}$ be a map over $G \subseteq \mathbb{R}^2$, $p, q \in \mathbb{N}$. The normalized central moments of order $(p+q)$ of f are defined as

$$\eta_{pq} = \frac{\mu_{pq}}{\mu_{00}^\gamma}, \qquad with \qquad \gamma = \frac{p+q+2}{2}.$$

Theorem 2.3.2 *(Scale Invariance)*
The normalized central moments η_{pq} of $f : G \to \mathbb{R}$, $G \subseteq \mathbb{R}^2$ are scale invariant, i.e. the values of η_{pq} do not vary under scaling of f by any factor $s \in \mathbb{R}\backslash\{0\}$.

Proof: Let $\tilde{f}$ be version of f scaled by a factor s, $s \in \mathbb{R}\backslash\{0\}$: $\tilde{f}(x,y) = f\left(\frac{x}{s}, \frac{y}{s}\right)$. Let the central moments be $\tilde{\mu}_{pq}$ and the normalized central moments be $\tilde{\eta}_{pq}$, both of order $(p+q)$ of $\tilde{f}$. As μ_{pq} is invariant under translation, one can choose the centroid to be placed in the origin. Then, the substitution $\lambda(x,y) = \left(\frac{x}{s}, \frac{y}{s}\right)^T$ yields:

$$\eta_{pq} = \frac{\mu_{pq}}{\mu_{00}^\gamma}$$

$$= \frac{\int_{-\infty}^{\infty}\int_{-\infty}^{\infty} x^p y^q f(x,y)\,dx\,dy}{\left(\int_{-\infty}^{\infty}\int_{-\infty}^{\infty} f(x,y)\,dx\,dy\right)^\gamma}$$

$$\lambda \stackrel{=}{=} \frac{\int\limits_{-\infty}^{\infty}\int\limits_{-\infty}^{\infty} \left(\frac{x}{s}\right)^p \left(\frac{y}{s}\right)^q f\left(\frac{x}{s},\frac{y}{s}\right) \left|\det\begin{pmatrix}\frac{1}{s} & 0 \\ 0 & \frac{1}{s}\end{pmatrix}\right| dxdy}{\left(\int\limits_{-\infty}^{\infty}\int\limits_{-\infty}^{\infty} f\left(\frac{x}{s},\frac{y}{s}\right) \left|\det\begin{pmatrix}\frac{1}{s} & 0 \\ 0 & \frac{1}{s}\end{pmatrix}\right| dxdy\right)^{\gamma}}$$

$$= \frac{\left(\frac{1}{s}\right)^{p+q+2} \int\limits_{-\infty}^{\infty}\int\limits_{-\infty}^{\infty} x^p y^q \tilde{f}(x,y) dxdy}{\left(\frac{1}{s}\right)^{2\gamma} \left(\int\limits_{-\infty}^{\infty}\int\limits_{-\infty}^{\infty} \tilde{f}(x,y) dxdy\right)^{\gamma}}$$

$$= \frac{\tilde{\mu}_{pq}}{\tilde{\mu}_{00}^{\gamma}} = \tilde{\eta}_{pq}$$

□

2.3.4 Rotation Invariance

Besides the recognition of patterns of varying scales the major issue is the recognition of rotated versions. This can be obtained using various approaches. Hu [Hu62], for example, proposed a set of moments that he derived algebraically in $\mathbb{R}$. Flusser [Flu00], however, has proven those moments to be neither independent nor complete. The most elegant formulation is probably the formulation of Flusser, using the complex moments to derive rotation invariance, as previously proposed by Mostafa and Psaltis [AMP84]. The following derivation of rotation invariant moments is connected to the work of Flusser [Flu00], since complex moments are utilized for the derivation. While Flusser concentrates just on the rotation property, the following paragraphs define rotation invariance based upon normalized central moments. First, the definition of scalar complex moments according to Flusser [Flu00] is given:

Definition 2.3.6 *(Scalar Complex Moments of order* $(p+q)$*)*
Let $f = f(x,y)$, $f : G \to \mathbb{R}$ *be a map over* $G \subseteq \mathbb{R}^2$, $p,q \in \mathbb{N}$, *and* $\mathrm{i} = \sqrt{-1} \in \mathbb{C}$. **Complex Moments** *of order* $(p+q)$ *of* f *are defined as*

$$c'_{pq} = \int\limits_{-\infty}^{\infty}\int\limits_{-\infty}^{\infty} (x+\mathrm{i}\,y)^p (x-\mathrm{i}\,y)^q f(x,y) dxdy.$$

2.3 Moment Invariants for Scalar Data

While the definitions of the previously presented translation and scale invariant moments can easily be adapted for arbitrary dimensions, this is not possible for complex moments. This formulation as well as the following derived properties hold only for the two dimensional case. By using the binomial theorem a connection between standard moments m_{pq} and c'_{pq} can be derived:

$$\begin{aligned}
c'_{pq} &= \int_{-\infty}^{\infty}\int_{-\infty}^{\infty} (x+\mathrm{i}\,y)^p (x-\mathrm{i}\,y)^q f(x,y)\,dx\,dy \\
&= \int_{-\infty}^{\infty}\int_{-\infty}^{\infty} \sum_{j=0}^{p}\binom{p}{j} x^j (\mathrm{i}\,y)^{p-j} \sum_{k=0}^{q}\binom{q}{k} x^k (-\mathrm{i}\,y)^{q-k} f(x,y)\,dx\,dy \\
&= \sum_{j=0}^{p}\sum_{k=0}^{q} \binom{p}{j}\binom{q}{k} (-1)^{q-k}\,\mathrm{i}^{p+q-j-k} \int_{-\infty}^{\infty}\int_{-\infty}^{\infty} x^{j+k} y^{p+q-j-k} f(x,y)\,dx\,dy \\
&= \sum_{j=0}^{p}\sum_{k=0}^{q} \binom{p}{j}\binom{q}{k} (-1)^{q-k}\,\mathrm{i}^{p+q-j-k} m_{j+k,p+q-j-k}
\end{aligned} \quad (2.1)$$

One can now formulate the complex moments based upon the normalized central moments yielding translation and scale invariant complex moments:

Definition 2.3.7 (Complex Normalized Central Moments of order $(p+q)$) *Let $f = f(x,y)$, $f : G \to \mathbb{R}$ be a map over $G \subseteq \mathbb{R}^2$, $p, q \in \mathbb{N}$, and $\mathrm{i} = \sqrt{-1} \in \mathbb{C}$. Let further $\gamma = \frac{p+q+2}{2}$, $\hat{x} = (x-\bar{x})$, and $\hat{y} = (y-\bar{y})$.* **Complex Normalized Central Moments** *of order $(p+q)$ of f are defined as*

$$c_{pq} = \frac{1}{\mu_{00}^\gamma} \int_{-\infty}^{\infty}\int_{-\infty}^{\infty} (\hat{x}+i\hat{y})^p (\hat{x}-i\hat{y})^q f(x,y)\,dx\,dy.$$

In analogy to (2.1), one can derive a connection between the normalized central moments η_{pq} and the complex normalized central moments c_{pq}:

$$c_{pq} = \sum_{j=0}^{p}\sum_{k=0}^{q} \binom{p}{j}\binom{q}{k} (-1)^{q-k}\,i^{p+q-j-k}\,\eta_{j+k,p+q-j-k}$$

A reformulation of c_{pq} in polar coordinates can be obtained by a substitution $\lambda(\hat{x}, \hat{y}) = (r\cos\varphi, r\sin\varphi)^T$:

$$c_{pq} = \int_0^\infty \int_0^{2\pi} r^{p+q+1} e^{i(p-q)\varphi} f(r\cos\varphi, r\sin\varphi) d\varphi dr.$$

This formulation in polar coordinates makes it possible to apply again a scaling operation, this time in angular terms. For obtaining rotation invariant moments the following Lemma has to be verified:

Lemma 2.3.1 *Let $\tilde{f}$ be a version of f, counter-clockwisely rotated around the origin with angle α: $\tilde{f}(r, \varphi) = f(r, \varphi - \alpha)$. Let $\tilde{c}_{pq}$ of order $(p+q)$ of $\tilde{f}$. Then it holds:*

$$\tilde{c}_{pq} = e^{i(p-q)\alpha} c_{pq}$$

Proof: Using the substitution $\lambda(r, \varphi) = (r, \varphi - \alpha)^T$ one obtains:

$$c_{pq} = \int_0^\infty \int_0^{2\pi} r^{p+q+1} e^{i(p-q)\varphi} f(r, \varphi) d\varphi dr$$

$$\stackrel{\lambda}{=} \int_0^\infty \int_\alpha^{2\pi+\alpha} r^{p+q+1} e^{i(p-q)(\varphi-\alpha)} f(r, \varphi - \alpha) \left| \det \begin{pmatrix} 1 & 0 \\ 0 & 1 \end{pmatrix} \right| d\varphi dr$$

$$= \int_0^\infty \int_0^{2\pi} r^{p+q+1} e^{i(p-q)(\varphi-\alpha)} \tilde{f}(r, \varphi) d\varphi dr$$

$$= e^{-i(p-q)\alpha} \underbrace{\int_0^\infty \int_0^{2\pi} r^{p+q+1} e^{i(p-q)\varphi} \tilde{f}(r, \varphi) d\varphi dr}_{\tilde{c}_{pq}}$$

$\square$

Having this Lemma, it is now obvious that items being independent of the rotation angle α can be formulated by a clever choice of p and q, so that the factor $e^{i(p-q)\alpha}$ is eliminated. For instance, it is automatically $c_{pp} = \tilde{c}_{pp}$ for $p \in \mathbb{N}$. The following theorem as equally formulated by Flusser [Flu00] shows how to generally derive

2.3 Moment Invariants for Scalar Data

scalar rotation invariant moments by combinations of certain $c_{p_j q_j}$, canceling out the dependence to α.

Theorem 2.3.3 (Construction of scalar rotation invariant moments)
Let $c_{p_j q_j}$ $(j = 1, ..., n)$ be complex moments of $f : G \to \mathbb{R}$, $G \subseteq \mathbb{R}^2$. If $\sum_{j=1}^{n}(p_j - q_j) = 0$, then

$$\Phi = \prod_{j=1}^{n} c_{p_j q_j}$$

is rotation invariant, i.e. the value of Φ does not vary under a rotation of f by any angle α.

Proof: Let $\tilde{f}$ be a version of f being rotated counter-clockwise around the origin by an angle α: $\tilde{f}(r, \varphi) = f(r, \varphi - \alpha)$. Let $\tilde{c}_{pq}$ be the complex moment of order $(p+q)$ of $\tilde{f}$. Then it holds:

$$\sum_{j=1}^{n}(p_j - q_j) = 0$$
$$\Rightarrow \sum_{j=1}^{n} i\,(p_j - q_j)\alpha = 0$$
$$\Leftrightarrow \prod_{j=1}^{n} e^{i(p_j - q_j)\alpha} = 1$$

Using Lemma 2.3.1 one obtains

$$\prod_{j=1}^{n} \tilde{c}_{p_j q_j} = \prod_{j=1}^{n} e^{i(p_j - q_j)\alpha} c_{p_j q_j} = \prod_{j=1}^{n} c_{p_j q_j}.$$

$\square$

As the derivation of rotation invariant moments has been based upon normalized central moments, moment invariants can be defined as follows:

Definition 2.3.8 *(Scalar Moment Invariants)*
Let $f = f(x,y)$, $f : G \to \mathbb{R}$ be a map over $G \subseteq \mathbb{R}^2$. Let $c_{p_j q_j}$ $(j = 1,...,n)$ be complex moments according to Definition (2.3.7). Then

$$\Phi = \prod_{j=1}^{n} c_{p_j q_j}, \quad \text{with} \quad \sum_{j=1}^{n}(p_j - q_j) = 0$$

is called a **Moment Invariant** of order $\max_{j=1,...,n} (p_j + q_j)$ of f. It is invariant to any translation, scaling, and rotation of f.

Using theorem 2.3.3 it is possible to generate an infinite number of moment invariants. These moment invariants can be depending on each other, so it makes sense to formulate minimal bases of moment invariants carrying the maximum information in a minimum number of elements.

2.3.5 Construction of an Invariant Moment Basis

The construction of an invariant moment basis of the herein presented moment invariants can be performed equally to the construction presented by Flusser [Flu00]. This section briefly summarizes the method as it is also important for the not yet discovered vector case.

Definition 2.3.9 *(Independence of Sets of Invariants)*
Let $\mathcal{I} = \{I_1, ..., I_k\}$, $k \geq 1$ be a set of invariants according to Definition 2.3.8 and let J be an invariant of the same type. The invariant J is said to be **dependent** on $\mathcal{I}$ if and only if there exists a function F with $J = F(I_1, ..., I_k)$ containing only the the operations multiplication, involution with an integer exponent, and complex conjugation. Otherwise, J is called **independent** from $\mathcal{I}$. Furthermore,

$\mathcal{I}$ is called **dependent**, if there exists an $I_j \in \mathcal{I}$, such that I_j is dependent on $\mathcal{I} - \{I_j\}$. Otherwise, $\mathcal{I}$ is called **independent**.

2.3 Moment Invariants for Scalar Data

Definition 2.3.10 *(Basis of a Set of Invariants)*
*Let $\mathcal{I}$ be a set of invariants according to Definition 2.3.8 and let $\mathcal{B} \subseteq \mathcal{I}$ be its subset. $\mathcal{B}$ is called **Basis** of $\mathcal{I}$ if and only if*

- *$\mathcal{B}$ is independent*

- *$\mathcal{B}$ is complete, i.e. if any element of $I \in \mathcal{I} - \mathcal{B}$ depends on $\mathcal{B}$.*

Using these two Definitions the Theorem for construction of moment invariant bases has been formulated by Flusser [Flu00], presenting a construction rule to generate bases for an arbitrary set of moment invariants.

Theorem 2.3.4 *(Construction of an Invariant Moment Basis for Scalar Fields)*
Let $\mathcal{M}$ be a set or a subset of the complex moments of any order c_{pq} of order $(p+q) \in \{0, ..., r\}$, with $r \geq 2$. Let $\mathcal{I}$ be the set of all invariants created from $\mathcal{M}$ according to Theorem 2.3.3. Let further be $c_{p_0 q_0} \in \mathcal{M}$, with $p_0 - q_0 = 1$ and $c_{p_0 q_0} \neq 0$. Then the set $\mathcal{B}$ constructed as

$$\mathcal{B} = \left\{ \Phi(p,q) := c_{pq} c_{q_0 p_0}^{p-q} \mid p \geq q \wedge c_{pq} \in \mathcal{M} \right\}$$

is a Basis of $\mathcal{I}$.

The proof of Theorem 2.3.4 can be found in [Flu00] for rotation invariants.

In practice, the fact that an invariant moment basis being independent and complete can be constructed strongly enhances the computation process. Only moments carrying non-redundant information are computed. On the other hand, with this construction rule also an infinite number of independent and complete sets of invariant bases can be computed, as the order $(p+q)$ can also be infinite. Therefore, in practice only lower order moments are computed for several reasons. One reason is that higher order moments become numerically unstable, as they would need more than *double*-precision to be computed accurately. A second reason is that lower order moments carry most of the information, similar to the low frequency band when regarding the Fourier space. Another argument for only regarding lower order moments for the application of pattern recognition is that higher order moments generate large amounts of data, and it is more efficient to pre-select possible pattern occurrences by lower order moments and check in detail only at those specific preselected positions rather than computing this large amount of data for the whole field. The pattern recognition method is explained in detail in chapter 6.

Using the centroid for translation invariance it yields $c_{01} = c_{10} = 0$, and a basis of all moment invariants of order ≤ 3 is given by

$$\mathcal{B} = \left\{ c_{00}, c_{11}, c_{21}c_{12}, c_{20}c_{12}^2, c_{30}c_{12}^3 \right\}$$

constructed according to Theorem 2.3.4 with $c_{p_0 q_0}$ chosen to be c_{21}.

While this section presented the theory of scalar moment invariants, most of it according to Flusser [Flu00], chapter 5 introduces a novel adaption of those moment invariants for flow data.

Chapter 3

State of the Art: Image Processing for Flow Visualization

The idea of *flow visualization* in general is to provide an insight into flow data by highlighting important features. As *image processing* provides well-engineered methods for feature extraction in images, those methods can obviously serve as basis for flow feature extraction.

A first approach aiming a convolution operator for flow data was proposed by Heiberg et al. [HEWK03]. Some extended approaches have been formulated by Ebling and Scheuermann using Clifford algebra. The field itself is quite immature, so these few approaches are the State-of-the-Art in *image processing for flow visualization*.

3.1 Clifford Convolution

The mentioned methods from section 2.2 have been reformulated to be applied to vector data. This means that vector valued filters can be applied to vector valued data. Using this mechanism it is possible to recognize certain query patterns in vector data. This mechanism works analogously to linear shift-invariant filtering in the scalar case.

Heiberg et al. defined the vector convolution using the scalar product [HEWK03]:

Definition 3.1.1 *Let V be a vector field and Q_n be a filter in direction n. The* ***inner convolution*** *is defined as*

$$s_n(r) = \int\int\int_\Omega \langle Q_n(\xi), V(r-\xi)\rangle \, d\xi.$$

We assume the filter to be the mirrored query pattern (for performing a correlation). Using terms of Clifford algebra the convolution was redefined by Ebling and Scheuermann [ES03]:

Definition 3.1.2 *Let U be a multi-vector field and P_n a multi-vector valued filter mask in direction n. The **Clifford convolution** is defined as*

$$c_n(r) = \int\int\int_\Omega P_n(\xi) U(r-\xi) |d\xi|$$

using the Clifford product.

In practice, discretized versions are needed. Here, the 2D case is of major interest, so 2D discretized definitions for inner and Clifford convolution are given:

Definition 3.1.3 *Let V be a vector field and Q_n be a filter in direction n. The 2D **discrete inner convolution** is defined as*

$$s_n(j,k) = \sum_{s=-r}^{r} \sum_{t=-r}^{r} \langle Q_n(s,t), V(j-s, k-t)\rangle$$

with $j, k, s, t \in \mathbb{Z}$.

Definition 3.1.4 *Let U be a multi-vector field and P_n a multi-vector valued filter mask in direction n. The **discrete Clifford convolution** is defined as*

$$c_n(j,k) = \sum_{s=-r}^{r} \sum_{t=-r}^{r} P_n(s,t) U(j-s, k-t)$$

with $j, k, s, t \in \mathbb{Z}$, using the Clifford multiplication.

3.1 Clifford Convolution

In this definition, the maximum size of the grid is r in any dimension. The definition is though universal, since filters having different sizes in different dimensions can be filled-up with zeros at the edges. Each (j, k, l) is representing a grid point. Besides the convolution operation, also the definition of the correlation operation can be extended to vector fields [HEWK03, ES03]:

Definition 3.1.5 *Let V be a vector field and Q_n be a filter in direction n. The **inner correlation** is defined as*

$$l_n(r) = \int \int \int_\Omega \langle Q_n(\xi), V(r+\xi) \rangle \, d\xi$$

Definition 3.1.6 *Let U be a multi-vector field and P_n a multi-vector valued filter mask in direction n. The **Clifford correlation** is defined as*

$$k_n(r) = \int \int \int_\Omega P_n(\xi) U(r+\xi) |d\xi|$$

The Clifford convolution is non-commutative, since the Clifford multiplication that it is based upon isn't either, so side from which a filter is applied is of importance.

Definition 3.1.7 *Let f be a multi-vector field and h be a multi-vector valued filter mask, both with dimension d. In addition to the definitions of the Clifford convolution and correlation*

$$(h *_l f)(x) = \int_{I\!R^d} h(x') f(x - x') |dx'|$$

*is defined as **left-side Clifford convolution**,*

$$(h \star_l f)(x) = \int_{I\!R^d} h(x') f(x + x') |dx'|$$

*is defined as **left-side Clifford correlation**,*

$$(f *_r h)(x) = \int_{\mathbb{R}^d} f(x - x')h(x')|dx'|$$

is defined as **right-side Clifford convolution**, and

$$(h \star_l f)(x) = \int_{\mathbb{R}^d} h(x')f(x + x')|dx'|$$

is defined as **right-side Clifford correlation**.

The discrete versions are defined analogously.

3.2 Pattern Matching on Vector Fields

The presented correlations can be used for pattern matching on vector fields. Pattern matching provides information about the features contained in the given vector data. Special features have characteristic pattern structures capable of being recognized by a correlation operation.

For one approach of the pattern matching a uniform grid structure is assumed for both, vector field and vector filter. The filters are defined through the discretized query patterns. Figure 3.2 shows some example patterns for two and three dimensions. In the pattern matching algorithms of Heiberg [HEWK03], as well as in the algorithm of Ebling and Scheuermann [ES03], the vector fields are normalized, meaning all vectors have the same length. This is done as the authors argue that direction of the vectors is more important than the vector length.

The application of one of the correlation operators from definition 3.1.5 or definition 3.1.7, results in a *similarity field*. This similarity field is a scalar field in Heiberg et al.'s case, while it is the scalar part of a multi-vector field in Ebling and Scheuermann's case. Both similarity fields indicate, where a given query pattern has been found in the field. Figure 3.2 illustrates this process. The major problem of this method is that the pattern can only be recognized in the given size and orien-

3.2 Pattern Matching on Vector Fields

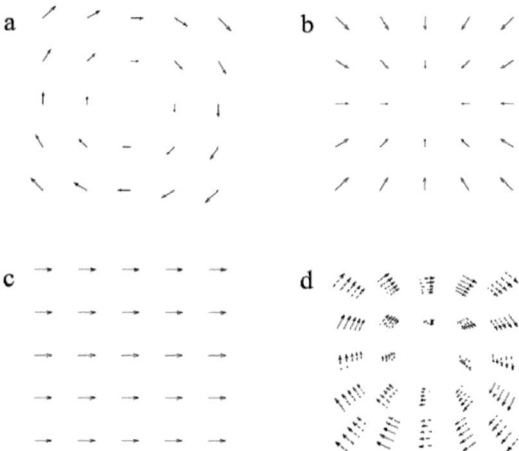

Figure 3.1: Some example vector patterns in 3D and 2D.

tation. For *easy* patterns being invariant to rotation and scale (like rotations, sinks, or sources), orientation and size are extraneous. In this case the application of the correlation operator directly results in a valuable information about these features.

However, for general patterns filters have to be redefined for different scales and for every of these scales in many different rotated versions, to guarantee a good result.

Heiberg et al. as well as Ebling and Scheuermann are concerned about rotations, not about scales. So, Heiberg defines the final similarity field $l(r)$ for each discrete position according to the most similar rotated version of the query pattern:

$$l(r) = \sup_n s_n(r).$$

Ebling and Scheuermann have extended their method to vector data on non-uniform grids [ES05a]. Most of their approaches use interpolation of the field and/or the filter to different grid structures. For their most successful approach, the filter grid

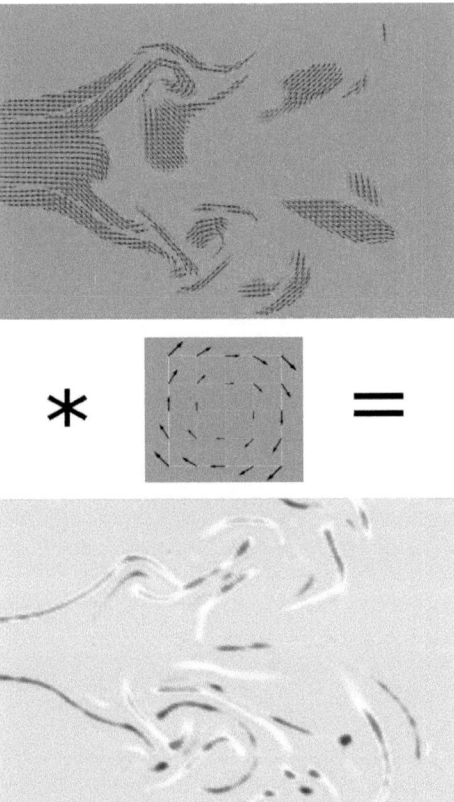

Figure 3.2: Pattern recognition on a flow simulation data set (data courtesy by W.Kollmann). The query pattern is a clock-wise rotation. Occurrences of the clockwise rotations and counter-clockwise rotations are highlighted in different colors in the resulting similarity field.

is adapted to the structure of the given field. This works very well for implicitly given query patterns that can be discretized easily. For explicitly given patterns again interpolation to the changed grid has to be used to perform the correlation. A similar approach using NFFT was presented in [SHN+05].

3.3 Clifford FFT

The correlation operator itself is very inefficient. Its complexity lies in $O(n^2)$, with n being the total number of data points. In the scalar case, the correlation is performed as a convolution of the mirrored filter using a fast Fourier transform (FFT) (see section 2.2.1).

There is indeed a FFT for the vector data. It is a extension of the approach of Ebling and Scheuermann using Clifford algebra. So, the FFT for vector data is called Clifford FFT [ES05b, Sch04].

For a Clifford FFT, first a general definition of the Clifford Fourier transform is needed, as in [Sch04].

Definition 3.3.1 : *Let $f : \mathbb{E}^d \to \mathcal{G}^d$ be a multi-vector valued function and vectors $x, u \in \mathbb{R}^d$. The **Clifford Fourier Transform** is defined by*

$$\mathcal{F}\{f\}(u) = \int_{\mathbb{R}^d} f(x) e^{(-2\pi i_d <x,u>)} |dx|$$

*and the **inverse Clifford Fourier Transform** is defined by*

$$\mathcal{F}^{-1}\{f\}(x) = \int_{\mathbb{R}^d} f(u) e^{(2\pi i_d <x,u>)} |du|$$

if the integral exists.

The properties are very similar to the scalar case. For further information on theorems and proofs for the Clifford Fourier transform, see [Sch04, ES05b]. For a fast Clifford Fourier transform the multi-vector field has to be decomposed:

For the 3D case, a multi-vector field $f : \mathbb{E}^3 \to \mathcal{G}^3$ can be decomposed into four complex signals:

$$\begin{aligned} f(x) &= [f_0(x) + f_{123}(x)i_3]1 \\ &+ [f_1(x) + f_{23}(x)i_3]e_1 \\ &+ [f_2(x) + f_{31}(x)i_3]e_2 \\ &+ [f_3(x) + f_{12}(x)i_3]e_3 \end{aligned}$$

Due to the linearity property of the Fourier transform it yields:

$$\begin{aligned} \mathcal{F}\{f\}(u) &= [\mathcal{F}_c\{f_0(x) + f_{123}(x)i_3\}(u)]1 \\ &+ [\mathcal{F}_c\{f_1(x) + f_{23}(x)i_3\}(u)]e_1 \\ &+ [\mathcal{F}_c\{f_2(x) + f_{31}(x)i_3\}(u)]e_2 \\ &+ [\mathcal{F}_c\{f_3(x) + f_{12}(x)i_3\}(u)]e_3. \end{aligned}$$

As the first Fourier pair uses scalar and trivector part (not being important for pure vector data), it can be dropped. The remaining three Fourier transforms are in fact three scalar Fourier transforms $\mathcal{F}_c$ each with one of the three vector components as input. This means that a Clifford Fourier transform can be calculated through scalar Fourier transforms, and thus, by FFTs.

For the 2D case the decomposition is similar. A multi-vector field $f : \mathbb{E}^2 \to \mathcal{G}^2$ can be decomposed into two complex signals:

$$\begin{aligned} f(x) &= 1[f_0(x) + f_{12}(x)i_2] \\ &+ e_1[f_1(x) + f_2(x)i_2] \end{aligned}$$

Using the linearity of the Fourier transform again yields

$$\begin{aligned} \mathcal{F}\{f\}(u) &= 1[\mathcal{F}_c\{f_0(x) + f_{12}(x)i_2\}(u)] \\ &+ e_1[\mathcal{F}_c\{f_1(x) + f_2(x)i_2\}(u)]. \end{aligned}$$

3.3 Clifford FFT

Again, non-vector data is located in the first Fourier transform (here scalar and bivector part). As those are zero for pure vector data, only the second Fourier transform is of interest. A Clifford Fourier transform can again be reduced to the scalar case and thus be calculated by an FFT algorithm. For pure vector data a scalar (but complex valued) Fourier transform suffice. The e_1 part is regarded as the real, while the e_2 part as the imaginary part fed into the Fourier transform.

To perform a correlation using the Clifford FFT, the convolution theorem also has to hold in Clifford algebra.

Theorem 3.3.1 *(Clifford Convolution Theorem): Let $f, h : \mathbb{E}^d \to \mathcal{G}^d$ be multi-vector valued functions of dimension d. If $\mathcal{F}\{f\}$ and $\mathcal{F}\{h\}$ exist then it is*

$$\mathcal{F}\{h *_l f\}(u) = \mathcal{F}\{h\}(u)\mathcal{F}\{f\}(u)$$

for the left-side Clifford convolution and

$$\mathcal{F}\{f *_r h\}(u) = \mathcal{F}\{f\}(u)\mathcal{F}\{h\}(u)$$

for the right-side Clifford convolution.

Proof: The proof is presented for the left-side convolution.

$$\begin{aligned}
&\mathcal{F}\{h *_l f\}(u) \\
&= \int_{\mathbb{R}^d} \int_{\mathbb{R}^d} h(x')f(x-x')|dx'|e^{(-2\pi i_d <x,u>)}|dx| \\
&= \int_{\mathbb{R}^d} \int_{\mathbb{R}^d} h(x')f(x-x')e^{(-2\pi i_d <x,u>)}|dx'||dx| \\
&= \int_{\mathbb{R}^d} \int_{\mathbb{R}^d} h(x')f(x-x')e^{(-2\pi i_d <x,u>)}|dx||dx'| \\
&= \int_{\mathbb{R}^d} h(x') \int_{\mathbb{R}^d} f(x-x')e^{(-2\pi i_d <x,u>)}|dx||dx'| \\
&= \int_{\mathbb{R}^d} h(x')e^{(-2\pi i_d <x',u>)}\mathcal{F}\{f\}(u)|dx'| \\
&= \int_{\mathbb{R}^d} h(x')e^{(-2\pi i_d <x',u>)}|dx'|\mathcal{F}\{f\}(u) \\
&= \mathcal{F}\{h\}(u)\mathcal{F}\{f\}(u).
\end{aligned}$$

50   State of the Art: Image Processing for Flow Visualization

The proof of the right-side convolution is analogue.

□

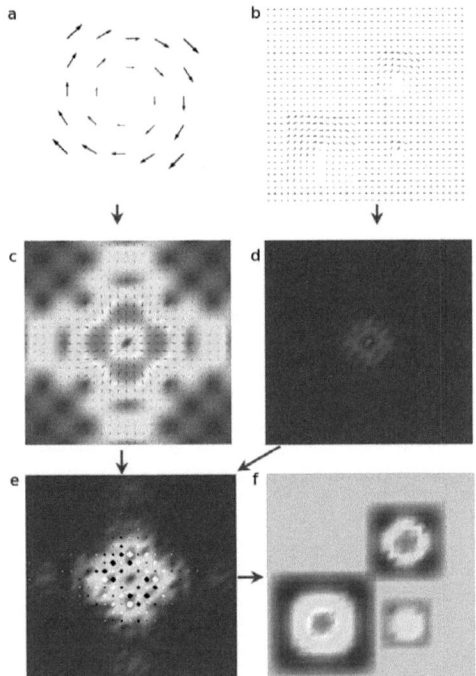

Figure 3.3: The complete pattern recognition process by using a Clifford FFT. The field and the filter mask (a+b) are transformed into frequency domain using the Clifford FFT (c+d). These are multiplied (e). The inverse Clifford FFT results in a similarity field (f). The example field contains three hidden rotation patterns. The filter mask of size 5x5 is able to produce good results for larger rotation patterns. A smaller rotation pattern is only recognized with lower similarity.

The convolution theorem offers the chance to perform pattern recognition much faster. For pattern recognition a correlation of the field with a query filter mask has to be performed. The correlation equals a convolution with the mirrored filter mask. The theorem says that a convolution in spatial domain equals a multiplication in frequency domain. Both, field and mirrored filter are transformed into frequency domain using the Clifford FFT, then multiplied, the result is transformed with the inverse Clifford FFT. The result is the similarity field. The complete process is visualized in Figure 3.3. This sounds quite complicated at first. But this process is very efficient (for filter sizes bigger than 3x3), since the complexity of a Clifford FFT lies in $O\left(n\ log_2(n)\right)$ and the complexity of the multiplication in $O(n)$, resulting in a total complexity of $O\left(n\ log_2(n)\right)$, with n being the number of data points in the field. This is a big improvement to the complexity of the common correlation operation with $O(n^2)$.

3.4 Open Questions

In this section some open questions are formulated that should be addressed in this book.

An important question addresses the analyzed data. As mentioned in section 2.1.1, there is a difference between different types of vector data. Although the Clifford correlation/convolution is defined for general vector data, it has yet only been used for the analysis of flow data.

- *How does the Clifford correlation / convolution behave on other vector data, for example color images?*

Besides these questions regarding the Clifford algebra approaches, the major issue that should be addressed is efficiency. Currently, it is very inefficient to perform a pattern recognition for general patterns. The correlation has to be performed several times for just one query pattern, as one can only find a query pattern in its scale and orientation with one correlation. Of course, a FFT improves efficiency, but it is still far away from interactive working (about 5-10 minutes for medium sized data sets for a complete search of a single general query pattern). The answer to this question can be a pattern recognition being independent from scale and orientation.

- *How can a flow pattern recognition be performed regardless from scale and orientation?*

During the process of pattern recognition one obtains a similarity field. Performing several searches yields several similarity maps. So far, these similarity maps are displayed as scalar data. For one similarity field, this can be done with a simple scalar color mapping in 2D, for 3D data with volume rendering. Visualizing more similarity fields, visibility problems occur immediately. Moreover, the original flow data cannot be displayed appropriately.

- *How can the results of the pattern recognition be displayed in the context of the original flow data?*

In part two of this work, the first question shall be addressed. Part three is dedicated to the central question of an efficient flow pattern recognition. Finally, part four presents a method being able to display the results in context of a flow visualization.

Part II

Extension of the Clifford-based Approach

Chapter 4

Color Edge Detection using Clifford Algebra

This chapter is dedicated to a different application of the Clifford Convolution and the Clifford Fourier Transform. The idea is to use the Clifford Fourier transform also in the context of *image processing* and *object recognition*. Segmentation based on *edge detection* is an important part of current classification systems in *image processing*. These systems are used in various application areas, including astronomy, medicine, robots, etc. *Edge detection* is usually the first step of the filtering process for images (see figure 2.1). Having the objects' edges, an image can be segmented into regions that can be classified with further methods with the goal of identifying objects and their characteristics from image data. This makes *edge detection* a vital part of the image processing pipeline.

4.1 Gray-scale Edge Detection

In most cases, edge detection is carried out on gray-scale images. It is performed by the convolution or correlation of special filter masks (as explained in 2.2.1). Edges in gray-scale images are (more or less) strong changes in the color value of pixels in a neighborhood. Thus, the basic idea of an edge detection in images is to utilize the gradients of an image. One method is to search for extreme values in the first-order derivatives. Since these extreme values are zero-crossings for second-order

4.1 Gray-scale Edge Detection

derivatives, a second method is to search for these zero-crossings. Assuming 2D images, the continuous gradient is defined as follows:

Definition 4.1.1 *Let* $g : \mathbb{R}^2 \to \mathbb{R}$ *be a two-dimensional signal. Its* **gradient** *is defined as*

$$\nabla g(x) = \left[\frac{\partial g}{\partial x_1}, \frac{\partial g}{\partial x_2}\right]^T.$$

According to Jähne [Jäh95], the absolute value of the gradient is invariant to a rotation of the coordinate system, and is thus a good choice for edge detection:

$$|\nabla g(x)| = \sqrt{\left(\frac{\partial g}{\partial x_1}\right)^2 + \left(\frac{\partial g}{\partial x_2}\right)^2}.$$

The corresponding discrete basis filter $\mathcal{D}$ is given by:

$$\mathcal{D} = \begin{bmatrix} D_x \\ D_y \end{bmatrix}, \quad \text{with the filter masks } D_x = [1 - 1] \text{ and } D_y = \begin{bmatrix} 1 \\ -1 \end{bmatrix}.$$

For isotropic edge detection, the discrete version of the absolute value of this filter is of importance ([Jäh95]):

$$|\mathcal{D}| = \sqrt{[D_x \cdot D_x + D_y \cdot D_y]},$$

with · being the point-wise multiplication of images.

For the second order method, the *Laplace operator* is applied. The following definition is a specialized version of the one from Jähne [Jäh95]:

Definition 4.1.2 *The* **Laplace operator** *for a 2D signal is defined as*

$$\Delta = \frac{\partial^2}{\partial x_1^2} + \frac{\partial^2}{\partial x_2^2}$$

The discrete Laplace operator (*Laplace filter*) can also be derived by applying the gradient operator twice [Jäh95]. The 2D *Laplace filter* is given by the following image matrix:

$$\mathcal{L} = \begin{bmatrix} 0 & 1 & 0 \\ 1 & -4 & 1 \\ 0 & 1 & 0 \end{bmatrix}.$$

These two presented methods are further optimized through smoothing operations and regularization to reduce the discretization error. Please note that it is not a discretized method that is introducing the error, but the discretely given image data. Examples for regularized filters are the *Sobel operator* (originally from a talk by Irwin Sobel 1968, published in a book of Duda and Hart [DH73]), the *Laplacian-of-Gauss filter* by Marr and Hildreth [MH80], and the *Canny edge detector* [Can86].

In the following sections, the basic principles of edge detection will be transferred to and carried out with the Clifford Fourier approach.

4.2 Color Edge Detection Approaches

There are also approaches for detection of edges using color information. Almost all of these approaches reduce the color edge detection to three scalar edge detections, e.g., the component-wise Canny edge detection is applied to each of the RGB color channels. To the author's knowledge there is only one really vector-based method from Machuca and Phillips [MP83]. Other methods are concentrating on optimization issues that are not relevant for this work. Most of these approaches have been discussed in the comparative overviews of color image edge detection methods from Koschan [Kos95] or a more recent one from Koschan and Abidi [KA05].

In order to improve color edge detection there is the idea of regarding RGB triples of colors as vectors, therefore the color image as vector field. Some standard image processing methods have been discussed in section 2.2 and section 4.1. Adaptations of these methods for vector field data, the *Clifford correlation* and the *Clifford Fourier transform*, have been illustrated in chapter 3. The idea of this chapter is to analyze the applicability of these methods to image data.

Definition 4.2.1 (*Color Image*) *A **color image** f is defined as a vector field $f : G \to \mathbb{R}^3$, $G \subseteq \mathbb{R}^2$. It assigns three-dimensional color values to a planar two-dimensional domain.*

4.3 Clifford Color Edge Detection

As color images can be represented as vector fields using the color components as vector components, the general idea of Clifford color edge detection is to use pattern matching for vector fields for the detection of edges in color images. The given 3D vectors (RGB) are on a 2D grid. The application of 3D pattern matching would lead to a 3D similarity map as result, being an inappropriate representation, since the result has to be projected back into two dimensions. For that reason, it is reasonable to handle luminance and chrominace separately. This can be achieved by transferring an *RGB image* to a corresponding *YUV image*. The Y channel represents the *luminance* (gray-scale image), while the *chrominance* is represented by the 2D vector field *UV*. After filtering, one obtains two scalar similarity maps that can be combined to a final similarity map representing edges in the color image. The gray-scale part *(Y)* can be treated exactly as done in the common approaches, and the pattern matching applied to the color part *(UV)* adds additional information. Machuca and Phillips [MP83] proposed similar settings for their method, but did not use Clifford algebra.

In this chapter it will be shown that using any of the filter masks used for representing special topological features (rotation, convergence, and divergence) allows one to detect edges in a color image. The 2D Clifford algebra is especially suitable for this task, since all components fit perfectly into the mathematical concept.

4.3.1 Data Structure

The Clifford multi-vectors in the 2D case are suitable for this approach. We can assign the values as follows:

name	grade	dimension	values
scalar	0	1	Y
vector	1	2	U, V
bivector	2	1	0

The Y component becomes the scalar part of our multi-vector at each grid position. The vector component is represented by UV, using U as real part with basis e_1 and V as imaginary part with basis e_2. The imaginary scalar part with basis $e_1 \wedge e_2$ is set to zero, as there is no imaginary component for the scalar part.

4.3.2 Choice of patterns

For the scalar part the choice of filters is simple, as it reduces to gray-scale edge detection. For the color component UV, the main question for using vector pattern matching is what patterns to search for. The topologically interesting features like rotation, divergence, and convergence are related to the gradient. To compute the *divergence* $\nabla \cdot v$ of a vector field v, the Clifford pattern matching approach can be used with a divergence pattern (see figure 4.1). To compute the *rotation* $|\nabla \times v|$ of a vector field v, a rotation pattern can be applied (see figure 4.1). For these reasons, these patterns seem to be reasonable choices for filtering the UV part. The four patterns that were used to perform the filtering are presented in Figure 4.1.

In addition, a blur filter can be applied prior to edge detection, as done in *Marr and Hildreths'* and *Canny*'s edge detection schemes [MH80, Can86]. It can be applied separately to all color channels, before converting an image to YUV, as well as to the YUV representation, since the conversion is a linear operation. An appropriate choice for these filters could enhance the final result.

4.3 Clifford Color Edge Detection

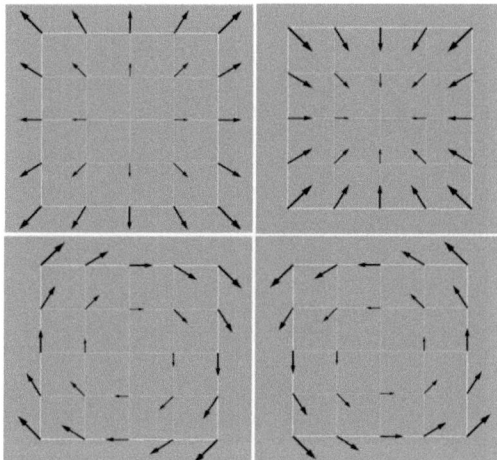

Figure 4.1: Four different vector pattern mask used as filters for the UV part: divergence (upper left), convergence (upper right), clockwise rotation (lower left) and counter-clockwise rotation (lower right).

4.3.3 The Detection Algorithm

The complete *Clifford color edge detection* process is illustrated in Figure 4.2. The RGB image is translated by a linear operation to a YUV image:

$$\begin{bmatrix} Y \\ U \\ V \end{bmatrix} = \begin{bmatrix} 0.299 & 0.587 & 0.114 \\ -0.14713 & -0.28886 & 0.436 \\ 0.615 & -0.51499 & -0.10001 \end{bmatrix} \begin{bmatrix} R \\ G \\ B \end{bmatrix}$$

More information on color models can be found for example in [Poy03].

After this transform, the gray-scale part *(Y)* is processed with usual edge detection, resulting in a similarity image revealing the gray-scale edges. The chrominance part *(UV)* is a two-dimensional vector field (but not flow field!). However, it is now filtered with one of the flow patterns from figure 4.1. The result is a complex similarity field. There are four different possibilities for edges:

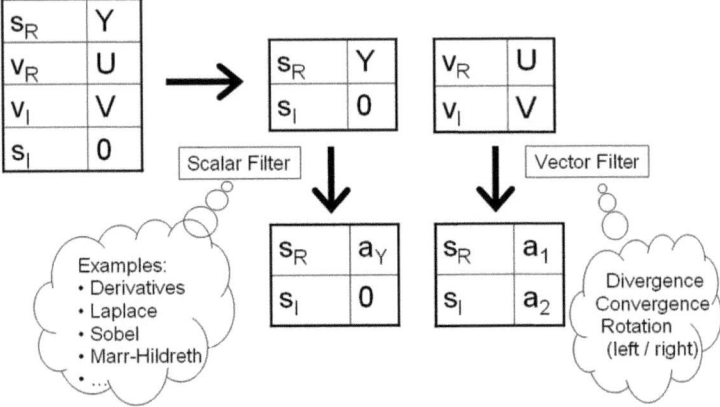

Figure 4.2: Illustration of Clifford color edge detection. Image given in YUV color space in a multi-vector structure, gray-scale edge detection performed as usual, UV part filtered with vector pattern matching. Result is a multi-vector of similarities.

- A horizontal edge from high to low values (up to down),
- a horizontal edge from low to high values (up to down),
- a vertical edge from high to low values (left to right), and
- a vertical edge from low to high values (left to right).

Each complex part of the resulting similarity field $a : \mathbb{R}^2 \to \mathbb{C}$ represents the result of one of these cases (positive real, positive imaginary, negative real, and negative imaginary part). Depending on the chosen pattern phase shifts do occur:

$$a\left(\nabla \cdot v\right) = i \cdot a\left(|\nabla \times v|\right).$$

The relation is obvious, when taking a look at the vector field from the perspective of complex numbers. The vector part of Clifford algebra is isomorph to .

Let $r : \mathbb{R}^2 \to \mathbb{C} \cong \mathbb{R}^2$ be the complex description of the clock-wise rotation pattern and $d : \mathbb{R}^2 \to \mathbb{C} \cong \mathbb{R}^2$ be the complex description of the divergence pattern as shown

4.3 Clifford Color Edge Detection

in figure 4.1. A point-wise multiplication with the phase shift i_2 means a clock-wise rotation of each single vector by 90 degrees:

$$r \cdot i_2 = d, \qquad d \cdot i_2 = -r, \qquad -r \cdot i_2 = -d, \qquad -d \cdot i_2 = r.$$

To conclude, the resulting similarity field does also only change its phase. Let $v' : \mathbb{R}^2 \to \mathbb{C} \cong \mathbb{R}^2$ be a complex scalar field being isomorph to the two-dimensional vector field v. Then:

$$a_r = v' * r = v' * d \cdot i_2 = a_d \cdot i_2.$$

Since the four complex parts have to be combined to give a full edge description, the absolute value of a is calculated. This means that the pattern can be chosen from any of the four proposed patterns, since

$$|\mathbf{a_r}| = |a_r \cdot i_2| = |\mathbf{a_d}| = |a_d \cdot i_2| = |-\mathbf{a_r}| = |-a_r \cdot i_2| = |-\mathbf{a_d}| = |-a_d \cdot i_2| = |\mathbf{a_r}|.$$

To recapitulate, given a color image, the algorithm computes two sets of similarity values: a set of real values and a set of complex values. The real set describes a fuzzy representation of the edges in the gray-scale image, while the magnitude of the complex value indicates edges in the color part of the image. The exact structure of the complex value depends on the used filter, but the unsigned magnitude of the complex similarity values turned out to be equal for all four filters that have been applied (two rotation pattern, a convergence, and a divergence pattern, see Figure 4.1).

4.3.4 Application Results

A software has been designed so that the user can adjust the binary threshold and the ratio of gray-scale and color contribution. It is possible to configure the identified edges as desired. For the presented algorithm, a chosen manual adjustment has been chosen, as the automatic thresholding problem known from Canny's algorithm [Can86] still applies to this case. Using the YUV model, users are able to control luminance and chrominance separately. This representation is more intuitive than a representation in RGB space, since the human sensory system processes luminance separately from chrominance.

Color Edge Detection using Clifford Algebra

Various images have been processed using this method. It generally performed better than simple gray-scale edge detection. Figure 4.3 shows an example where a gray-scale recognition fails. Examples for real-world image data are shown in Figures 4.4, 4.5, and 4.6. The enhancement using our color approach is illustrated by comparison with the common gray-scale algorithm.

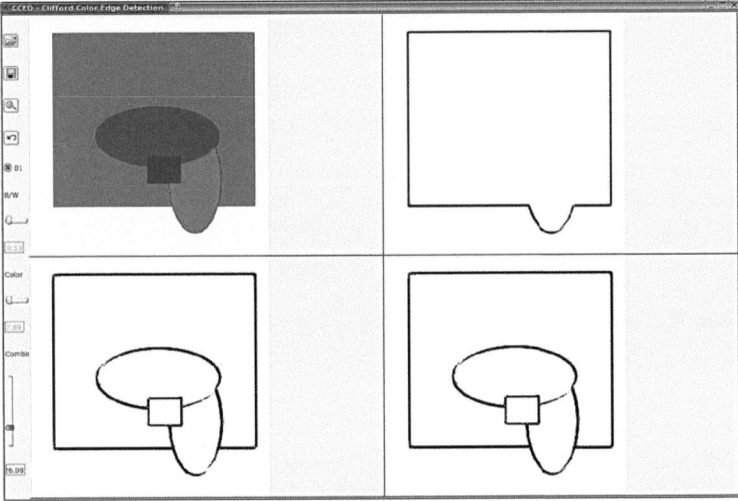

Figure 4.3: Example where gray-scale edge detection fails, while color edge detection succeeds. Upper left: (contrast enhanced) original image, upper right: result of a gray-scale edge detection, lower left: the color edge detection, lower right: the combined edge detection, showing all edges in the original image.

The presented algorithm turns out to be equal in performance to an optimally configured color edge detection method using the RGB color model. The transformation from RGB into YUV space does not change the result when all component results are weighted equally. The vector-based approach in Clifford algebra for handling the UV part is an operation applied to complex-valued scalars. Those can again be rewritten component-wise, splitting them into a real and an imaginary part. Rewriting the vector filter pattern (see Figure 4.1) in components yields the commonly used filters for edge detection for scalar images in both axis directions. The four different types of filters only differ in their algebraic signs for the real and imaginary values.

Since in the final step of the algorithm the magnitude of the complex result is computed, the search pattern can be either one of the given ones to obtain the same result.

Figure 4.4: C²ED applied to example image, resulting in a fuzzy representation of the similarity values. Upper left: original, upper right: Y filtered, lower left: UV filtered, lower right: weighted combination of Y and UV parts

4.4 Conclusions

This chapter presented an alternative method for color image edge detection for color images using Clifford algebra. Gray-scale data is handled separately from the color part of the image. While the luminance part is handled using common methods the color part is filtered with a vector-valued filter. Those two approaches fit perfectly in the data structure of Clifford algebra's multi-vector setting. The results have shown that this approach outperforms the gray-scale edge detection in most cases, since additional information is gained through the processing of the color part. However, it turned out to be equal in performance when compared to other color edge detection methods working component-wise on RGB images. For non-automatic detection, a framework has been implemented that offers the possibility to adjust thresholds manually. For manual adjustment the chosen YUV color model is more intuitive.

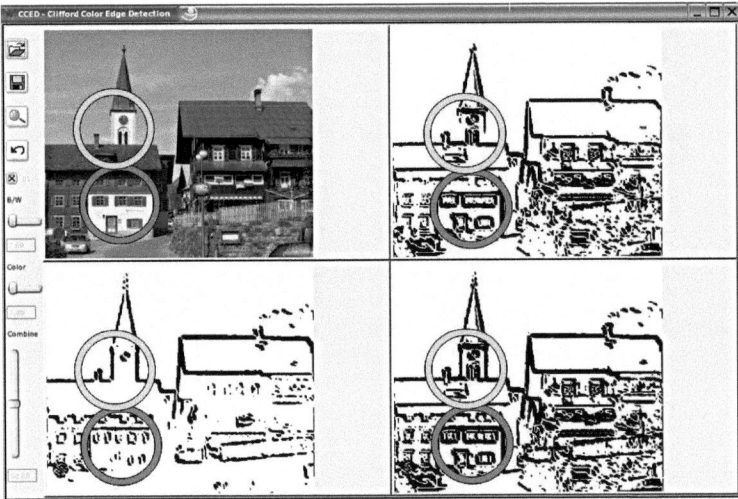

Figure 4.5: This image shows a street and a church tower in Gaschurn, Austria. Upper left: original, upper right: Y filtered, lower left: UV filtered, lower right: weighted combination of Y and UV parts. The church tower edges are only fully recognized using both, luminance and chrominance part. Also the window edges of the house on the left have been detected better.

4.4 Conclusions

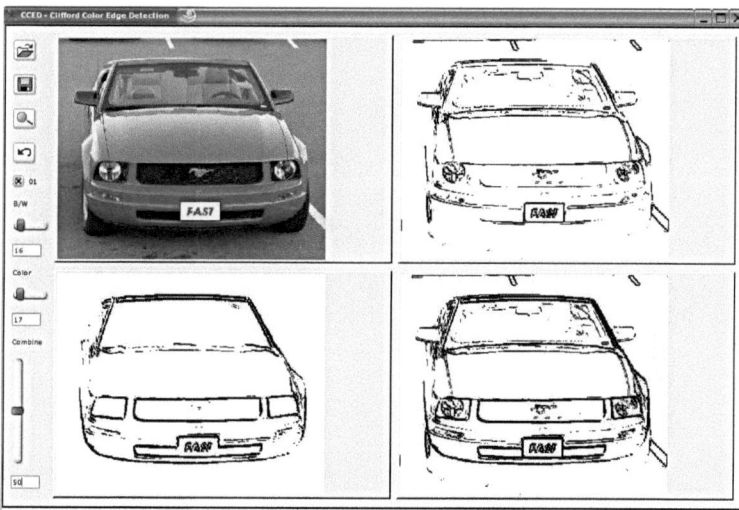

Figure 4.6: For this image of a car (upper left) thresholding was performed, resulting in a binary edge representation (upper right: Y, lower left: UV, lower right: combined). Results can be further improved using Canny's method.

Part III

Flow Pattern Recognition using Moment Invariants

Chapter 5

Generalized Moment Invariants

This chapter introduces *flow moment invariants* as foundation for an interactive pattern recognition algorithm for flow data. As previously described, the correlation operation is enabling pattern recognition in scalar and vector valued data. As shown, the process of correlation can be optimized by performing a Fourier Transform and a multiplication with the mirrored filter mask in frequency domain. The correlation method itself is especially good in finding patterns that are rotation invariant, i.e. rotations, convergence, and divergence patterns. For arbitrary patterns, however, the search pattern has to be adapted for different orientations. Also the scale has to be taken account. So, a pattern recognition seeking arbitrary patterns in flow data has to compute correlations for all possible scales and, for each of these scales, several discretely rotated versions of the search pattern. Even though using the presented optimization, this task slows down the search process heavily. The idea to overcome this issue is to develop a descriptor representing information independent from scale and rotation.

In the areas of *image processing* and *computer vision* the *moment invariants* serve as descriptor for parts of images with the property of invariance to translation, scaling, and rotation. In this chapter a generalization of these Moment Invariants is presented.

A novel definition of moment invariants for 2D flow fields will be given. It differs significantly from the original version (see section 2.3), since a component-wise application is not applicable for flows. In section 5.4 the characteristics of this new descriptor for special flow features are presented. The novel pattern search algorithm that has been developed based upon these descriptors is discussed in detail in chapter 6.

5.1 Definition of Moment Invariants for Flow Data

While the presented scalar moment invariants are known descriptors (see section 2.3), there is no descriptor for flow data, yet. When generalizing moment invariants to flow fields it is not sufficient to consider each component separately as it would be possible for spatially uncorrelated vector-valued data, e.g., color images. The definition of rotation invariance of scalar moment invariants is not appropriate for flow fields. The main issue here is the rotation operation. Component-wise application of moments only considers the rotation of the vector start positions, but for flow patterns also the vector values have to be taken into account. This problem is illustrated in an example shown in figure 5.1. In the following paragraph the math-

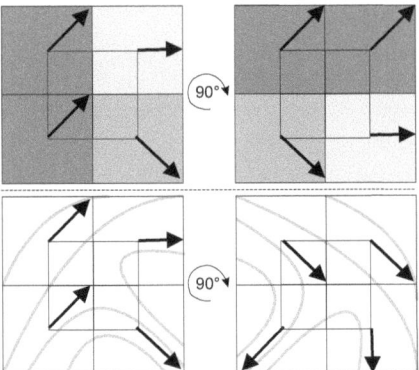

Figure 5.1: Difference in the understanding of a rotation operation between spatially uncorrelated data (e.g., a vector representation of colors, (upper part) and flow data (lower part). While for uncorrelated data a rotation only applies to the domain, rotation of the (vector) values has to be taken into account for an invariant description of flow features.

5.1 Definition of Moment Invariants for Flow Data

ematical foundations of flow moment invariants are explained. As an example for application areas of moment invariants, section 5.4 shows the characteristics of moment invariants for critical point features. For this special area, moment invariants are quite similar to other known descriptors like the Pointcare index. In contrast to the Pointcare index, moments are designed to handle more general patterns, not only critical point features.

5.1.1 Moments for Flows

In the following flow moments are defined for two-dimensional flow fields. Those flow fields are given by a two-dimensionally valued map $f : G \to \mathbb{R}^2$ over a two-dimensional domain $G \subseteq \mathbb{R}^2$. Moments of flow fields can be defined as follows:

Definition 5.1.1 (Moments of 2D Vector Fields)
Let $f = \begin{pmatrix} f_1(x,y) \\ f_2(x,y) \end{pmatrix}$, $f : G \to \mathbb{R}^2$ be a map over $G \subseteq \mathbb{R}^2$, let $p, q \in \mathbb{N}$ and $i = \sqrt{-1} \in \mathbb{C}$. A **Moment** of order $(p+q)$ of f is defined as

$$m_{pq} = \int_{-\infty}^{\infty}\int_{-\infty}^{\infty} x^p y^q f_1(x,y) dx dy + i \int_{-\infty}^{\infty}\int_{-\infty}^{\infty} x^p y^q f_2(x,y) dx dy$$

$$= \int_{-\infty}^{\infty}\int_{-\infty}^{\infty} x^p y^q \left(f_1(x,y) + i\, f_2(x,y) \right) dx dy \in \mathbb{C}.$$

The moment m_{pq} is defined component-wise. The real part of m_{pq} contains the moment of order $(p+q)$ of the first component of f while its imaginary part contains the second one. The definition has been chosen to be over $\mathbb{C}$ rather than $\mathbb{R}^2$, since this will be of importance for the derivation of rotation invariant moments.

5.1.2 Translation Invariance

In section 2.3.2 it has been explained that one can use the gray-scale centroid as origin to guarantee translation invariance for images. However, this can not be adapted for flow fields. One possibility would be to use the vector length to obtain a centroid, similar to a gray-scale centroid. In this case, however, the vector length have a very strong impact on the invariance and is not suitable when regarding homogenized vector fields. Using the vector directions to determine a centroid entails two problems. The minor issue that summed up direction values result in negative values or zero, and might not relate to the given domain, might be solved by clever shifting operations. The major issue, however, mapping the periodic direction values onto a non-periodic domain implies a gap in the definition of invariance. I.e., there is no fair solution for mapping a constellation of periodically defined directions onto a limited non-periodic domain.

For the scalar case an alternative centroid definition was given by using the characteristic function (see section 2.3.2). For flow fields the characteristic function can be defined as follows:

Definition 5.1.2 (Characteristic Function of a Flow Field)
Let $f = \begin{pmatrix} f_1(x,y) \\ f_2(x,y) \end{pmatrix}$, $f : G \to \mathbb{R}^2$ be map over $G \subseteq \mathbb{R}^2$. The **characteristic function** $\chi_f : G \to \{0,1\}$ of f is defined as

$$\chi_f(x,y) = \begin{cases} 1 & , \text{ if } f(x,y) \neq (0,0)^T \\ 0 & , \text{ if } f(x,y) = (0,0)^T \end{cases}.$$

The position of f can be replaced by the position of χ_f. If f is translated by a vector $v = (v_1, v_2) \in \mathbb{R}^2$, χ_f is also translated by this vector. Using this definition it is possible to transform the global coordinated into local coordinates, as shown in the scalar case. The resulting centroid will be written as $(\bar{x}, \bar{y}) \in \mathbb{R}^2$ in the following. Similar to the scalar case one can define translation invariant central moments.

5.1 Definition of Moment Invariants for Flow Data

Definition 5.1.3 (Central Moments for Flows)
Let $f = \begin{pmatrix} f_1(x,y) \\ f_2(x,y) \end{pmatrix}$, $f : G \to \mathbb{R}^2$ be a map over $G \subseteq \mathbb{R}^2$ and χ_f its characteristic function, and $p, q \in \mathbb{N}$. The **central moment** of order $(p+q)$ of f is defined as

$$\mu_{pq} = \int_{-\infty}^{\infty} \int_{-\infty}^{\infty} (x - \bar{x})^p (y - \bar{y})^q \left(f_1(x,y) + \mathrm{i}\, f_2(x,y) \right) dx dy \in \mathbb{C},$$

with

$$\bar{x} = \frac{\int_{-\infty}^{\infty} \int_{-\infty}^{\infty} x \cdot \chi_f(x,y) dx dy}{\int_{-\infty}^{\infty} \int_{-\infty}^{\infty} \chi_f(x,y) dx dy} \quad \text{and} \quad \bar{y} = \frac{\int_{-\infty}^{\infty} \int_{-\infty}^{\infty} y \cdot \chi_f(x,y) dx dy}{\int_{-\infty}^{\infty} \int_{-\infty}^{\infty} \chi_f(x,y) dx dy}$$

being the coordinates of the centroid of χ_f, and thus the centroid of f.

With the following theorem the translation invariance of central moments is proven.

Theorem 5.1.1 (Translation Invariance)
The central moments μ_{pq} of $f : G \to \mathbb{R}^2$, $G \subseteq \mathbb{R}^2$ are invariant to translation, i.e. their value does not change with a translation of f by any vector $v = (v_1, v_2) \in \mathbb{R}^2$.

Proof: Let $\tilde{f}$ be a copy of f being translated with translation vector v: $\tilde{f}(x,y) = f(x-v_1, y-v_2)$. Then, $\tilde{\mu}_{pq}$ is the central moment of order $(p+q)$ of $\tilde{f}$. The centroid of $\chi_{\tilde{f}}$ is according to definition 5.1.3 defined as $(\bar{x} + v_1, \bar{y} + v_2)$. The statement can be proven by using the substitution $\lambda(x,y) = (x - v_1, y - v_2)^T$:

$$\mu_{pq} = \int_{-\infty}^{\infty} \int_{-\infty}^{\infty} (x - \bar{x})^p (y - \bar{y})^q f(x,y) dx dy$$

$$\stackrel{\lambda}{=} \int_{-\infty}^{\infty} \int_{-\infty}^{\infty} (x - v_1 - \bar{x})^p (y - v_2 - \bar{y})^q f(x-v_1, y-v_2) \left| \det \begin{pmatrix} 1 & 0 \\ 0 & 1 \end{pmatrix} \right| dx dy$$

$$= \int_{-\infty}^{\infty} \int_{-\infty}^{\infty} (x - (\bar{x} + v_1))^p (y - (\bar{y} + v_2))^q \tilde{f}(x,y) dx dy$$

$$= \tilde{\mu}_{pq}$$

$\square$

The central moments for vector data can also be calculated by using regular vector moments m_{pq} as given in Definition 5.1.1:

$$\mu_{pq} = \sum_{j=0}^{p} \sum_{k=0}^{q} \binom{p}{j} \binom{q}{k} (-\bar{x})^{p-j} (-\bar{y})^{q-k} m_{jk}. \tag{5.1}$$

5.1.3 Scale Invariance

Scale invariance can be developed based upon the translation invariant central moments. In contrast to scalar moments, two cases have to be distinguished. This is, because the scaling operation itself can be defined differently. In the following *total scaling* is used as term for a scaling operation scaling both, domain and vector length. The term used for an operation only scaling the domain and not the vector length is *domain scaling*. Figure 5.2 illustrates these two scaling possibilities. For the purpose of pattern recognition it is reasonable to split up the recognition process to control parameters separately. Thus, it makes sense to regard only directions, i.e. a homogenized version of a vector field, research the similarity of certain patterns in directional manners, and then proceed by comparing the vector lengths separately. For this purpose homogenized vector fields with the notion of domain scaling are suitable. On the other hand if one is only interested in flow patterns matching exactly, i.e. versions being scaled in domain and vector length equally, a scale invariance based upon total scaling makes sense. For each scaling operation moments being scale invariant can be defined.

Another issue in defining scale invariant moments for flow fields is that in contrast to scalar fields a normalization by a specific power of the volume of the field cannot be used, since there is no specific volume of a vector field. The solution is again the characteristic function χ_f as given in Definition 5.1.2. Since χ_f scales in the same way as the original function f does, the volume of χ_f can be used to define scale invariance.

5.1.3.1 Domain Scale Invariance

In the following, a definition of a domain scale invariant is given. Moreover, specific normalized central moments for flows are given and proven to be domain scale invariant.

Definition 5.1.4 *Let* $f : G \to \mathbb{R}^2$, $G \subseteq \mathbb{R}^2$ *Let further* $\tilde{f} : \tilde{G} \to \mathbb{R}^2$ *be a version of* f, *on a domain scaled by a factor* $s \in \mathbb{R}\backslash\{0\}$: $\tilde{f}(x,y) = f(\frac{x}{s}, \frac{y}{s})$. *An invariant* I_s *with* $I_s(f) = I_s(\tilde{f})$ *is called domain scale invariant.*

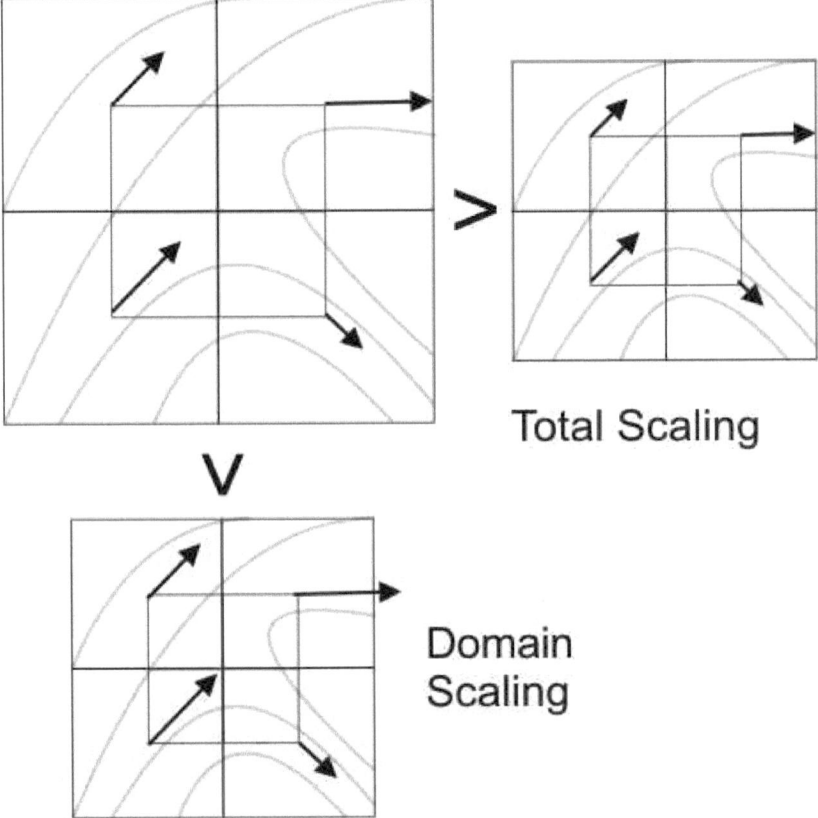

Figure 5.2: Two different scaling operations. For domain scaling only positions, not the vector values are scaled. For total scaling positions and values are scaled equally.

5.1 Definition of Moment Invariants for Flow Data

The following definition and theorem reveal the construction of domain scale invariant moments using the a power of the volume of χ_f as normalization factor.

Definition 5.1.5 (Domain Specific Normalized Central Moments)
Let $f = (f_1(x,y), f_2(x,y))^T$, $f: G \to \mathbb{R}^2$ be a map over $G \subseteq \mathbb{R}^2$, and $p, q \in \mathbb{N}$. The domain specific normalized central moments of order $(p+q)$ are defined as

$$\eta_{pq}^{(d)} = \frac{\mu_{pq}}{V(\chi_f)^\gamma}, \quad \text{with} \quad V(\chi_f) = \int_{-\infty}^{\infty}\int_{-\infty}^{\infty} \chi_f(x,y) dx dy$$

$$\text{and} \quad \gamma = \frac{p+q+2}{2}.$$

Theorem 5.1.2 (Domain Scale Invariance of Moments)
Let $f = (f_1(x,y), f_2(x,y))^T$, $f: G \to \mathbb{R}^2$ a map over $G \subseteq \mathbb{R}^2$ and χ_f its characteristic function. Let be $p, q \in \mathbb{N}$ and $V(\chi_f)$ the volume of χ_f over G. Then the domain specific normalized central moments $\eta_{pq}^{(d)}$ of order $(p+q)$ are domain scale invariants, i.e. they do not change under domain scaling of f by any factor $s \in \mathbb{R}\setminus\{0\}$.

Proof: Let $\tilde{f}$ be version of f domain scaled by a factor s, $s \in \mathbb{R}\setminus\{0\}$: $\tilde{f}(x,y) = f\left(\frac{x}{s}, \frac{y}{s}\right)$. Let the central moments be $\tilde{\mu}_{pq}$ and the normalized central moments be $\tilde{\eta}_{pq}$, both of order $(p+q)$ of $\tilde{f}$. As μ_{pq} is invariant under translation, one can choose the centroid to be placed in the origin. Then, the substitution $\lambda(x,y) = \left(\frac{x}{s}, \frac{y}{s}\right)^T$ yields:

$$\eta_{pq}^{(d)} = \frac{\mu_{pq}}{V(\chi_f)^\gamma}$$

$$= \frac{\int_{-\infty}^{\infty}\int_{-\infty}^{\infty} x^p y^q f(x,y) dx dy}{\left(\int_{-\infty}^{\infty}\int_{-\infty}^{\infty} \chi_f(x,y) dx dy\right)^\gamma}$$

$$\stackrel{\lambda}{=} \frac{\int_{-\infty}^{\infty}\int_{-\infty}^{\infty} \left(\frac{x}{s}\right)^p \left(\frac{y}{s}\right)^q f\left(\frac{x}{s},\frac{y}{s}\right) \left|\det\begin{pmatrix}\frac{1}{s} & 0 \\ 0 & \frac{1}{s}\end{pmatrix}\right| dx dy}{\left(\int_{-\infty}^{\infty}\int_{-\infty}^{\infty} \chi_f\left(\frac{x}{s},\frac{y}{s}\right) \left|\det\begin{pmatrix}\frac{1}{s} & 0 \\ 0 & \frac{1}{s}\end{pmatrix}\right| dx dy\right)^\gamma}$$

$$= \frac{\left(\frac{1}{s}\right)^{p+q+2} \int\limits_{-\infty}^{\infty} \int\limits_{-\infty}^{\infty} x^p y^q \tilde{f}(x,y) dx dy}{\left(\frac{1}{s}\right)^{2\gamma} \left(\int\limits_{-\infty}^{\infty} \int\limits_{-\infty}^{\infty} \chi_{\tilde{f}}(x,y) dx dy\right)^{\gamma}}$$

$$= \frac{\tilde{\mu}_{pq}}{V(\chi_{\tilde{f}})^{\gamma}} = \tilde{\eta}_{pq}^{(d)}$$

□

5.1.3.2 Total Scale Invariance

The second case of scale invariance is regarding not only the position of the vectors, but also their values. For the application of pattern recognition this kind of invariance can be used for a more restrictive distinction. In the following, total scale invariance is defined.

Definition 5.1.6 *Let $f: G \to \mathbb{R}^2$, $G \subseteq \mathbb{R}^2$ Let further $\tilde{f}: \tilde{G} \to \mathbb{R}^2$ be a version of f, scaled by a factor $s \in \mathbb{R}\backslash\{0\}$ in domain and value: $\tilde{f}(x,y) = s \cdot f(\frac{x}{s}, \frac{y}{s})$. An invariant I_s with $I_s(f) = I_s(\tilde{f})$ is called total scale invariant.*

The following definition and theorem reveal the construction of total scale invariant moments, again using the a power of the volume of χ_f as normalization factor.

Definition 5.1.7 (Totally Normalized Central Moments)
Let $f = (f_1(x,y), f_2(x,y))^T$, $f: G \to \mathbb{R}^2$ be a map over $G \subseteq \mathbb{R}^2$, and $p, q \in \mathbb{N}$. The totally normalized central moments of order $(p+q)$ are defined as

$$\eta_{pq}^{(t)} = \frac{\mu_{pq}}{V(\chi_f)^{\gamma}}, \quad \text{with} \quad V(\chi_f) = \int\limits_{-\infty}^{\infty} \int\limits_{-\infty}^{\infty} \chi_f(x,y) dx dy$$

$$\text{and} \quad \gamma = \frac{p+q+3}{2}.$$

Theorem 5.1.3 (Total Scale Invariance of Moments)
Let $f = (f_1(x,y), f_2(x,y))^T$, $f: G \to \mathbb{R}^2$ a map over $G \subseteq \mathbb{R}^2$ and χ_f its characteristic function. Let be $p, q \in \mathbb{N}$ and $V(\chi_f)$ the volume of χ_f over G. Then the domain specific normalized central moments $\eta_{pq}^{(t)}$ of order $(p+q)$ are total scale invariants, i.e. they do not change under total scaling of f by any factor $s \in \mathbb{R}\backslash\{0\}$.

5.1 Definition of Moment Invariants for Flow Data

Proof: Let $\tilde{f}$ be version of f domain scaled by a factor s, $s \in \mathbb{R}\backslash\{0\}$: $\tilde{f}(x,y) = s \cdot f\left(\frac{x}{s}, \frac{y}{s}\right)$. Let the central moments be $\tilde{\mu}_{pq}$ and the normalized central moments be $\tilde{\eta}_{pq}$, both of order $(p+q)$ of $\tilde{f}$. As μ_{pq} is invariant under translation, one can choose the centroid to be placed in the origin. Then, the substitution $\lambda(x,y) = \left(\frac{x}{s}, \frac{y}{s}\right)^T$ yields:

$$\eta_{pq}^{(t)} = \frac{\mu_{pq}}{V(\chi_f)^\gamma}$$

$$= \frac{\int\limits_{-\infty}^{\infty}\int\limits_{-\infty}^{\infty} x^p y^q f(x,y) dx dy}{\left(\int\limits_{-\infty}^{\infty}\int\limits_{-\infty}^{\infty} \chi_f(x,y) dx dy\right)^\gamma}$$

$$\stackrel{\lambda}{=} \frac{\int\limits_{-\infty}^{\infty}\int\limits_{-\infty}^{\infty} \left(\frac{x}{s}\right)^p \left(\frac{y}{s}\right)^q f\left(\frac{x}{s}, \frac{y}{s}\right) \left|\det\begin{pmatrix}\frac{1}{s} & 0 \\ 0 & \frac{1}{s}\end{pmatrix}\right| dx dy}{\left(\int\limits_{-\infty}^{\infty}\int\limits_{-\infty}^{\infty} \chi_f\left(\frac{x}{s}, \frac{y}{s}\right) \left|\det\begin{pmatrix}\frac{1}{s} & 0 \\ 0 & \frac{1}{s}\end{pmatrix}\right| dx dy\right)^\gamma}$$

$$= \frac{\left(\frac{1}{s}\right)^{p+q+3} \int\limits_{-\infty}^{\infty}\int\limits_{-\infty}^{\infty} x^p y^q \tilde{f}(x,y) dx dy}{\left(\frac{1}{s}\right)^{2\gamma} \left(\int\limits_{-\infty}^{\infty}\int\limits_{-\infty}^{\infty} \chi_{\tilde{f}}(x,y) dx dy\right)^\gamma}$$

$$= \frac{\tilde{\mu}_{pq}}{V(\chi_{\tilde{f}})^\gamma} = \tilde{\eta}_{pq}^{(t)}$$

□

5.1.4 Complex Flow Moments

The derivation of rotation invariant flow moment invariants is similar to the scalar case based on complex moments, as used by Flusser [Flu00]. In the following, the complex moments c'_{pq} are generalized to vector-valued functions.

Definition 5.1.8 (Complex Moments for Flows)
Let $f : \mathbb{R}^2 \to \mathbb{C} \cong \mathbb{R}^2$ be a map from $\mathbb{R}^2$ with $f \neq 0$ only in a compact subset $G \subseteq \mathbb{R}^2$. Let further $p, q \in \mathbb{N}$ and $i = \sqrt{-1} \in \mathbb{C}$. The complex moment of order $(p+q)$ of f is defined as

$$c'_{pq} = \int_{-\infty}^{\infty} \int_{-\infty}^{\infty} (x+iy)^p (x-iy)^q f(x,y) dx dy.$$

Note, that the isomorphism of $\mathbb{R}^2$ and $\mathbb{C}$ is used to represent the image of f as complex values. By application of the binomial theorem complex moments of arbitrary order can be represented as linear combinations of regular moments:

$$c'_{pq} = \sum_{j=0}^{p} \sum_{k=0}^{q} \binom{p}{j} \binom{q}{k} (-1)^{q-k} i^{p+q-j-k} m_{j+k, p+q-j-k}$$

These complex moments based upon regular moments m_{pq} are not yet invariant to translation and scaling. By appropriate shifting and scaling operations according to the previous sections 5.1.2 and 5.1.3 one can define translation and scale invariant complex moments.

Definition 5.1.9 (Complex Normalized Central Moments for Flows)
The normalized complex central flow moments of order $(p+q)$ are defined as

$$c_{pq} = \frac{1}{v^\gamma} \int_{-\infty}^{\infty} \int_{-\infty}^{\infty} (\hat{x}+i\hat{y})^p (\hat{x}-i\hat{y})^q f(x,y) dx dy$$

with $v = V(\chi_f) = \int_G 1\, dx dy$, $\hat{x} = (x - \bar{x})$, $\hat{y} = (y - \bar{y})$, and $\gamma = \frac{p+q+3}{2}$ for total scale invariance, $\gamma = \frac{p+q+2}{2}$ for domain scale invariance.

5.1 Definition of Moment Invariants for Flow Data

An alternative representation for c_{pq} is again derived by application of the binomial theorem. It reveals its connection to normalized central moments η_{pq}:

$$c_{pq} = \sum_{j=0}^{p} \sum_{k=0}^{q} \binom{p}{j}\binom{q}{k} (-1)^{q-k} \, i^{p+q-j-k} \, \eta_{j+k,p+q-j-k} \qquad (5.2)$$

with the normalized central moments

$$\eta_{pq} = \frac{1}{v^\gamma} \int_{-\infty}^{\infty} \int_{-\infty}^{\infty} \hat{x}^p \hat{y}^q f(x,y) dx dy. \qquad (5.3)$$

This connection proves the complex normalized central flow moments c_{pq} to be translation and scale invariant. Rotation invariance can now be constructed based upon these complex normalized central flow moments.

5.1.5 Rotation Invariance

For the derivation of rotational invariance it is essential to rewrite the moments in polar form. This can be done similarly for regular complex moments c'_{pq} as well as the translation and scale invariant version c_{pq}. Since the derivation of rotation invariance is independent of scale- and translation-invariance, only the term *complex moments* is used, as it is more general. The substitutions of $\hat{x} = r\cos(\varphi)$ and $\hat{y} = r\sin(\varphi)$ yield

$$c_{pq} = \frac{1}{v^\gamma} \int_0^\infty \int_0^{2\pi} r^{p+q+1} \, e^{i(p-q)\varphi} \, f(r,\varphi) d\varphi dr. \qquad (5.4)$$

This is the polar form of the complex flow moments. Using this polar form it is easy to derive the following Lemma:

Lemma 5.1.1 *Let $f : \mathbb{R}^2 \to \mathbb{C} \cong \mathbb{R}^2$ be a map from $\mathbb{R}^2$ with $f \neq 0$ only in a compact subset $G \subseteq \mathbb{R}^2$ and let $\tilde{f} : \mathbb{R}^2 \to \mathbb{C} \cong \mathbb{R}^2$ be a version of f rotated around its centroid with angle α: $\tilde{f}(r,\varphi) = e^{i\alpha} \cdot f(r, \varphi - \alpha)$. Let further $p, q \in \mathbb{N}$ and $i = \sqrt{-1} \in \mathbb{C}$, c_{pq} and $\tilde{c}_{pq}$ the complex moments of order $(p+q)$ of f and $\tilde{f}$, respectively. Then:*

$$\tilde{c}_{pq} = e^{i(p-q+1)\alpha} \, c_{pq} \qquad (5.5)$$

Proof: Using the substitution $\lambda(r,\varphi) = (r, \varphi-\alpha)^T$ one obtains:

$$c_{pq} = \frac{1}{v^\gamma} \int_0^\infty \int_0^{2\pi} r^{p+q+1} e^{i(p-q)\varphi} f(r,\varphi) d\varphi dr$$

$$\stackrel{\lambda}{=} \frac{1}{v^\gamma} \int_0^\infty \int_\alpha^{2\pi+\alpha} r^{p+q+1} e^{i(p-q)(\varphi-\alpha)} f(r,\varphi-\alpha) d\varphi dr$$

$$= e^{-i(p-q+1)\alpha} \underbrace{\frac{1}{v^\gamma} \int_0^\infty \int_0^{2\pi} r^{p+q+1} e^{i(p-q)\varphi} \tilde{f}(r,\varphi) d\varphi dr}_{\tilde{c}_{pq}}$$

$$= e^{-i(p-q+1)\alpha} \tilde{c}_{pq}$$

$\square$

Using this lemma, a set of moments being invariant to rotations for 2D flow fields can be derived. For this purpose, the factor $e^{i(p-q+1)\alpha}$ has to be eliminated by an appropriate combination of complex moments c_{pq}.

Theorem 5.1.4 (Construction of rotation-invariant moments)
Let $c_{p_j q_j}$, $j = 1,...,n$, be complex moments of a map $f: G \to \mathbb{C} \cong \mathbb{R}^2$, with $G \subseteq \mathbb{R}^2$ and let $\sum_{j=1}^{n}(p_j - q_j) = -n$. Then

$$I_r = \prod_{j=1}^{n} c_{p_j q_j} \tag{5.6}$$

is invariant under rotation, i.e., I_r does not change when f is rotated with an arbitrary angle α.

Proof: Let $\tilde{f}$ be a rotated version of f (counter-clockwise around the origin), i.e., $\tilde{f}(r,\varphi) = f(r, \varphi - \alpha)$ where α is the angle of rotation. Further let the complex moment of the order $(p+q)$ of $\tilde{f}$ be denoted as $\tilde{c}_{pq}$. One can derive the following:

$$\sum_{j=1}^{n}(p_j - q_j) = -n \quad \Leftrightarrow \quad \sum_{j=1}^{n}(p_j - q_j + 1) = 0$$

5.1 Definition of Moment Invariants for Flow Data

$$\Rightarrow \sum_{j=1}^{n} i(p_j - q_j + 1)\alpha = 0 \quad \Leftrightarrow \quad \prod_{j=1}^{n} e^{i(p_j - q_j + 1)\alpha} = 1$$

and with Lemma 5.1.1 it follows

$$\prod_{j=1}^{n} \tilde{c}_{p_j q_j} = \prod_{j=1}^{n} e^{i(p_j - q_j + 1)\alpha} c_{p_j q_j} = \prod_{j=1}^{n} c_{p_j q_j}.$$

$\square$

According to this theorem moment invariants for flow fields can be defined as follows:

Definition 5.1.10 (Moment Invariants for Flow Fields)
Let $f : G \to \mathbb{R}^2$ be a map over $G \subseteq \mathbb{R}^2$. Let further $c_{p_j q_j}$ $(j = 1, ..., n)$ be complex normalized central flow moments as presented in Definition 5.1.9. Any Ψ constructed as follows:

$$\Psi = \prod_{j=1}^{n} c_{p_j q_j}, \quad \text{with} \quad \sum_{j=1}^{n} (p_j - q_j) = -n$$

is called **Moment Invariant** (translation, scale, and rotation invariant) of order $\max_{j=1,...,n} (p_j + q_j)$ of f.

5.1.6 Construction of an Invariant Moment Basis for Flows

A combination of complex moments needs to satisfy the property $\sum_{j=1}^{n}(p_j - q_j) = -n$ as stated in Theorem 5.1.4 to form moment invariants. Using the shown methods to derive translation-, scale- and rotation-invariant moments, an infinite number of moment invariants can be generated. In practical applications, only a finite number can be used. In scalar application, moments are in general limited to order three, since higher-order moments become more and more numerically instable due to discretization. Furthermore, almost all information is stored in lower-order moments. As also explained in chapter 2.3.4 it makes sense to in practice restrict the computation to moments of lower order. For flow moments it can be restricted to moments of order two or order three. To avoid the computation of redundant information again bases for moment invariants can be constructed. The basic definitions needed for the construction are formulated analogously to the scalar case:

Definition 5.1.11 (Independence of Sets of Invariants)
Let $\mathcal{I} = \{I_1, ..., I_k\}$, $k \geq 1$ be a set of invariants according to Definition 5.1.10 and let J be an invariant of the same type. The invariant J is said to be **dependent** on $\mathcal{I}$ if and only if there exists a function F with $J = F(I_1, ..., I_k)$ containing only the the operations multiplication, involution with an integer exponent, and complex conjugation. Otherwise, J is called **independent** from $\mathcal{I}$. Furthermore,

$\mathcal{I}$ is called **dependent**, if there exists an $I_j \in \mathcal{I}$, such that I_j is dependent on $\mathcal{I} - \{I_j\}$. Otherwise, $\mathcal{I}$ is called **independent**.

Definition 5.1.12 (Basis of a Set of Invariants)
Let $\mathcal{I}$ be a set of invariants according to Definition 5.1.10 and let $\mathcal{B} \subseteq \mathcal{I}$ be its subset. $\mathcal{B}$ is called **Basis** of $\mathcal{I}$ if and only if

- $\mathcal{B}$ is independent

- $\mathcal{B}$ is complete, i.e. if any element of $I \in \mathcal{I} - \mathcal{B}$ depends on $\mathcal{B}$.

The construction of an invariant moment basis for flows turns out to be a little more complicated than for the scalar case. Therefore, two lemmas have two be formulated prior to the construction theorem. The formulation of these lemmas and the theorem was joint work with Heringer [Her07].

Lemma 5.1.2 Let $a : \mathbb{Z} \to \mathbb{N}$ and $b : \mathbb{Z} \to \mathbb{N}$ be sequences, and $m \in \mathbb{Z}$ with

$$a_m = \begin{cases} 0 & , \text{if } m \geq -1 \\ (|m| + 1) \text{ div } 3 & , \text{if } m \leq -2 \end{cases}$$

and

$$b_m = \begin{cases} m + 1 & , \text{if } m \geq -1 \\ (m + 1) \bmod 3 & , \text{if } m \leq -2 \end{cases}.$$

Then it holds:

$$3a_m - b_m = -m - 1$$

5.1 Definition of Moment Invariants for Flow Data

Proof: [Her07] Case differentiation of possible values for m:

- **Case 1:** $m \leq -2 \Rightarrow |m| = -m$

  - **Case 1.1:** $m \bmod 3 = 0$
  $$\begin{aligned} & 3\left[(-m+1) \text{ div } 3\right] - \left[(m+1) \bmod 3\right] \\ = & 3\left[\frac{-m+1}{3} - \frac{1}{3}\right] - 1 \\ = & -m+1-1-1 = -m-1 \end{aligned}$$

  - **Case 1.2:** $m \bmod 3 = 1$
  $$\begin{aligned} & 3\left[(-m+1) \text{ div } 3\right] - \left[(m+1) \bmod 3\right] \\ = & 3\left[\frac{-m+1}{3}\right] - 2 \\ = & -m+1-2 = -m-1 \end{aligned}$$

  - **Case 1.3:** $m \bmod 3 = 2$
  $$\begin{aligned} & 3\left[(-m+1) \text{ div } 3\right] - \left[(m+1) \bmod 3\right] \\ = & 3\left[\frac{-m+1}{3} - \frac{2}{3}\right] - 0 \\ = & -m+1-2 = -m-1 \end{aligned}$$

- **Case 2:** $m \geq -1$
  $$3 \cdot 0 - (m+1) = -m-1$$

$\square$

Figure 5.3 gives a graphical illustration of the conclusion of Lemma 5.1.2.

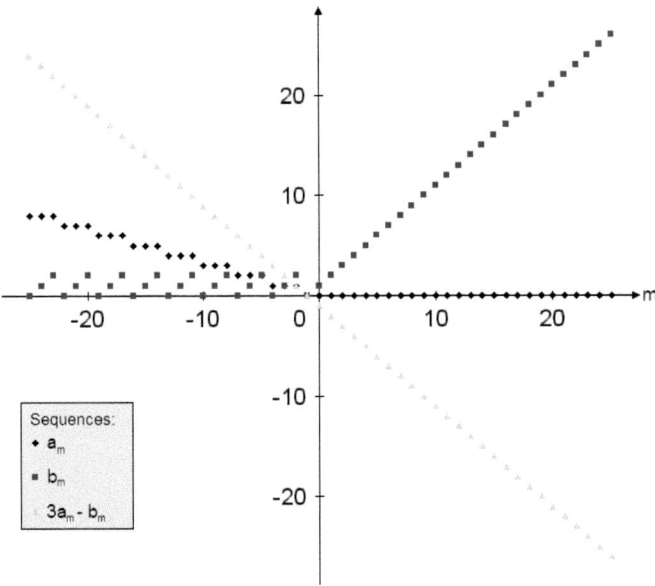

Figure 5.3: Graphical illustration of Lemma 5.1.2 [Her07].

Lemma 5.1.3 *Let $a : \mathbb{Z} \to \mathbb{N}$ and $b : \mathbb{Z} \to \mathbb{N}$ be sequences as given in Lemma 5.1.2 and let $\sum_{j=1}^{n}(p_j - q_j) = -n$. Then it is*

$$3\sum_{j=1}^{n} a_{p_j - q_j} = \sum_{j=1}^{n} b_{p_j - q_j}$$

5.1 Definition of Moment Invariants for Flow Data

Proof: [Her07] Using $\Delta_j := p_j - q_j$ as abbreviation one obtains:

$$3\sum_{j=1}^{n} a_{\Delta_j} = \sum_{j=1}^{n} b_{\Delta_j}$$

$$\Leftrightarrow \quad \sum_{j=1}^{n}\left(3a_{\Delta_j} - b_{\Delta_j}\right) = 0$$

$$\stackrel{\text{Lemma 5.1.2}}{\Leftrightarrow} \quad \sum_{j=1}^{n}(-\Delta_j - 1) = 0$$

$$\Leftrightarrow \quad \underbrace{-\sum_{j=1}^{n}\Delta_j - \sum_{j=1}^{n} 1}_{-n} = 0$$

$$\Leftrightarrow \quad -(-n) - n = 0$$

$$\Leftrightarrow \quad 0 = 0$$

$\square$

Using the Lemmas 5.1.2 and 5.1.3 the invariant basis for flow data can be constructed.

Theorem 5.1.5 (Construction of a Basis for Flow Moment Invariants)
Let $\mathcal{M}$ be the set or a subset of all complex moments c_{pq} of order $(p+q) \in \{0, ..., r\}$, $r \geq 2$. Let $\mathcal{I}$ be the set of all moment invariants being constructed according to equation (5.6) from elements of $\mathcal{M}$. Let be $c_{\dot{p}\dot{q}}$ and $c_{\ddot{p}\ddot{q}} \in \mathcal{M}$, with $\dot{p} - \dot{q} = \ddot{q} - \ddot{p} = 2$ and $c_{\dot{p}\dot{q}}$ as well as $c_{\ddot{p}\ddot{q}} \neq 0$. If the set $\mathcal{B}$ is constructed as follows:

$$\mathcal{B} = \left\{\Psi(p,q) := c_{pq} c_{\dot{p}\dot{q}}^{a_{p-q}} c_{\ddot{p}\ddot{q}}^{b_{p-q}} \mid c_{pq} \in \mathcal{M}\right\},$$

with
$$a_m = \begin{cases} 0 & , \text{if } m \geq -1 \\ (|m|+1) \text{ div } 3 & , \text{if } m \leq -2 \end{cases}$$

and
$$b_m = \begin{cases} m+1 & , \text{if } m \geq -1 \\ (m+1) \text{ mod } 3 & , \text{if } m \leq -2 \end{cases}$$

Then $\mathcal{B}$ is a basis of $\mathcal{I}$.

Proof: [Her07] *Completeness of $\mathcal{B}$*:
Let $I \in \mathcal{I}$, i.e. $I = \prod_{j=1}^{n} c_{p_j q_j}$, with $\sum_{j=1}^{n}(p_j - q_j) = -n$ and $c_{p_j q_j} \in \mathcal{M}$.
The construction of J is performed using only values from $\mathcal{B}$ as follows:

$$J = \prod_{j=1}^{n} \Psi(p_j, q_j) = \prod_{j=1}^{n} c_{p_j q_j} c_{\dot{p}\dot{q}}^{a_{p_j-q_j}} c_{\ddot{p}\ddot{q}}^{b_{p_j-q_j}}$$

Grouping of $c_{\dot{p}\dot{q}}$ and $c_{\ddot{p}\ddot{q}}$ yields

$$J = c_{\dot{p}\dot{q}}^{\sum_{j=1}^{n} a_{p_j-q_j}} c_{\ddot{p}\ddot{q}}^{\sum_{j=1}^{n} b_{p_j-q_j}} \prod_{j=1}^{n} c_{p_j q_j} = c_{\dot{p}\dot{q}}^{\sum_{j=1}^{n} a_{p_j-q_j}} c_{\ddot{p}\ddot{q}}^{\sum_{j=1}^{n} b_{p_j-q_j}} I.$$

Since I is required to be an invariant ($I \in \mathcal{I}$), it is $\sum_{j=1}^{n}(p_j - q_j) = -n$. Using Lemma 5.1.3 yields:

$$3 \sum_{j=1}^{n} a_{p_j-q_j} = \sum_{j=1}^{n} b_{p_j-q_j}$$

Defining $K := \sum_{j=1}^{n} a_{p_j-q_j}$, J can be written as

$$J = c_{\dot{p}\dot{q}}^{K} c_{\ddot{p}\ddot{q}}^{3K} I = \left(c_{\dot{p}\dot{q}} c_{\ddot{p}\ddot{q}}^{3}\right)^{K} I.$$

According to the requirements it is $\dot{p} - \dot{q} = 2$. Thus, it is

$$\Psi(\dot{p}, \dot{q}) = c_{\dot{p}\dot{q}} c_{\ddot{p}\ddot{q}}^{3}.$$

Finally, I can be written only with elements from $\mathcal{B}$:

$$I = \frac{J}{\Psi(\dot{p}, \dot{q})^{K}}$$

meaning that $\mathcal{B}$ is complete.

Independence of $\mathcal{B}$:
Proof by contradiction: Assuming $\mathcal{B}$ being dependent, i.e. there is an $\Psi(p, q) \in \mathcal{B}$, being dependent to $\mathcal{B} - \{\Psi(p, q)\}$. It is obvious that this element from $\mathcal{B}$ has to be element of $\Psi(\dot{p}, \dot{q})$ or $\Psi(\ddot{p}, \ddot{q})$. This is because any other pair (p, q) is applied in exactly one basis element as c_{pq}. It can, due to the independence of complex moments

5.1 Definition of Moment Invariants for Flow Data 87

according to Definition 5.1.8, neither be represented by other complex moments $c_{p_j q_j}$, nor by a combination of elements of $\mathcal{B} - \{\Psi(p,q)\}$. In the following the dependent element is assumed to be $\Psi(\dot{p},\dot{q})$. Then there exist invariants $\Psi(p_1,q_1), ..., \Psi(p_m,q_m)$ and $\Psi(s_1,s_1), ..., \Psi(s_n,s_n)$ from $\mathcal{B} - \{\Psi(\dot{p},\dot{q})\}$, with which one is able to construct $\Psi(\dot{p},\dot{q})$ only by application of the operations multiplication and involution with an integer exponent (see Definition 5.1.11), i.e. it can be written as

$$\Psi(\dot{p},\dot{q}) = \frac{\prod_{i=1}^m \Psi(p_i,q_i)}{\prod_{j=1}^n \Psi(s_j,t_j)} = \frac{\prod_{i=1}^m c_{p_i q_i} c_{\dot{p}\dot{q}}^{a_{p_i-q_i}} c_{\ddot{p}\ddot{q}}^{b_{p_i-q_i}}}{\prod_{j=1}^n c_{s_j t_j} c_{\dot{p}\dot{q}}^{a_{s_j-t_j}} c_{\ddot{p}\ddot{q}}^{b_{s_j-t_j}}}.$$

Grouping of $c_{\dot{p}\dot{q}}$ and $c_{\ddot{p}\ddot{q}}$ yields

$$\Psi(\dot{p},\dot{q}) = \underbrace{\frac{c_{\dot{p}\dot{q}}^{\sum_{i=1}^m a_{p_i-q_i}}}{c_{\dot{p}\dot{q}}^{\sum_{j=1}^n a_{s_j-t_j}}}}_{A} \cdot \underbrace{\frac{c_{\ddot{p}\ddot{q}}^{\sum_{i=1}^m b_{p_i-q_i}}}{c_{\ddot{p}\ddot{q}}^{\sum_{j=1}^n b_{s_j-t_j}}}}_{B} \cdot \underbrace{\frac{\prod_{i=1}^m c_{p_i q_i}}{\prod_{j=1}^n c_{s_j t_j}}}_{C}.$$

According to the requirements, it is $\dot{p} - \dot{q} = 2$. It follows

$$\Psi(\dot{p},\dot{q}) = c_{\dot{p}\dot{q}} c_{\ddot{p}\ddot{q}}^3.$$

This means, the exponents of A or B have to be

$$K_A := \sum_{i=1}^m a_{p_i-q_i} - \sum_{j=1}^n a_{s_j-t_j} = 1 \qquad (5.7)$$

and

$$K_B := \sum_{i=1}^m b_{p_i-q_i} - \sum_{j=1}^n b_{s_j-t_j} = 3 \qquad (5.8)$$

respectively.
Moreover, it is $C = 1$. Due to the given independence of the complex moments it follows that

$$m = n$$
$$p_i = s_i$$
$$q_i = t_i$$

for each i.

However, application of these constraints to equations (5.7) and (5.8) yields

$$K_A = 0$$
$$K_B = 0,$$

being a contradiction.

In case of the assumption the dependent element was $\Psi(\ddot{p}, \ddot{q})$, a contradiction can be derived analogously.

$\square$

For the application of pattern recognition a basis $\mathcal{B}$ of order three of invariant moments can be constructed, according to Theorem 5.1.5, incorporating translation, scale, and rotation invariance. The basis of the set of all moment invariants $\mathcal{B}$ of order ≤ 3 for flow vector moment invariants can be defined as

$$\mathcal{B}_3 = \left\{ c_{01}, c_{00}c_{02}, c_{11}c_{02}, c_{10}c_{02}^2, c_{20}c_{02}^3, c_{12}, c_{21}c_{02}^2, c_{03}c_{20}c_{02}, c_{30}c_{02}^4 \right\}$$

according to Theorem 5.1.5. While $c_{\dot{p}\dot{q}}$ has been chosen to be c_{02}, $c_{\ddot{p}\ddot{q}}$ has been chosen to be c_{20}. The basis of the set of all moment invariants $\mathcal{B}_3$ of order ≤ 3 for flow vector moment invariants can be defined as

$$\mathcal{B}_2 = \left\{ c_{01}, c_{00}c_{02}, c_{11}c_{02}, c_{10}c_{02}^2, c_{20}c_{02}^3 \right\}.$$

being a subset of $\mathcal{B}_3$, also with $c_{\dot{p}\dot{q}}$ being c_{02} and $c_{\ddot{p}\ddot{q}}$ being c_{20}). For improved notation in the following sections, the following abbreviations for the complex-valued basis elements are defined (see also [SHM+07]):

$$\begin{aligned}
\Psi_1 &= c_{01}, \\
\Psi_2 &= c_{00}c_{02}, \\
\Psi_3 &= c_{11}c_{02}, \\
\Psi_4 &= c_{10}c_{02}^2, \\
\Psi_5 &= c_{20}c_{02}^3.
\end{aligned} \quad (5.9)$$

5.2 Critical Point Characteristics of Flow Moments

The development of the independent and complete basis for the flow moment invariants as defined in chapter 5.1.1 makes it possible to efficiently apply them to flow fields. Before developing the pattern recognition algorithm, there are some fundamental questions to answer on the behavior of flow moment invariants on flow data. Since flow data is often analyzed and visualized using topological approaches as described in section 2.1.1, it is important to know about the behavior of this new descriptor on critical point features. With the information derived in the following paragraphs, it is possible to give an efficient algorithm for finding critical point features using flow moment invariants, being presented in section 6.2. This paragraph exemplarily provides some continuous moment representations for prototypical 2D critical points. This continuous evaluation is compared with the discrete computation results in section 6.2. Critical points are only a special class of patterns to be observed in connection with moment invariants. However, it is reasonable to consider them as a good example to show how the moments are evaluated continuously and provide some information on their behavior.

Exemplarily, the calculation of the continuous flow moment invariant values for a counter-clockwise rotation pattern is presented. The pattern can be described continuously by $f : G \to \mathbb{R}^2$:

$$f(x, y) = \begin{cases} (0, 0)^T & \text{, if } x = y = 0 \\ \frac{1}{\sqrt{x^2+y^2}} \begin{pmatrix} -y \\ x \end{pmatrix} & \text{, otherwise} \end{cases} \quad (5.10)$$

The moments of f over a circular domain with radius one and center in the critical point can be derived with equation (5.1.4):

$$m_{pq} = \int_{-1}^{1} \int_{-\sqrt{1-x^2}}^{\sqrt{1-x^2}} x^p y^q \frac{-y + \mathrm{i}\, x}{\sqrt{x^2 + y^2}} dy dx \quad (5.11)$$

Generalized Moment Invariants

source / divergence	sink / convergence	axis drain
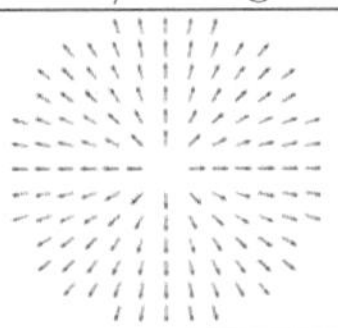	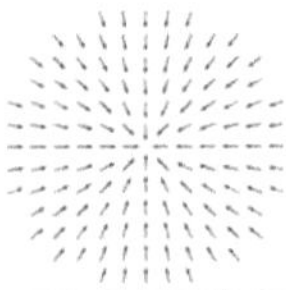	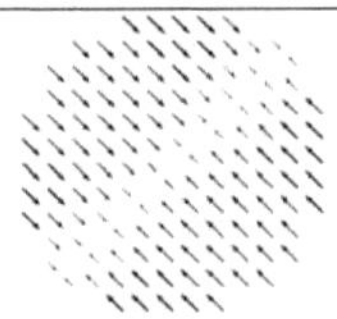
$\Psi_1 = \frac{2}{3\sqrt{\pi}}$ $\Psi_{2,3,4,5} = 0$	$\Psi_1 = -\frac{2}{3\sqrt{\pi}}$ $\Psi_{2,3,4,5} = 0$	$\Psi_1 = -\frac{2}{3\sqrt{\pi}}\frac{2}{\pi}$ $\Psi_{2,3,4,5} = 0$
counter-clockwise rotation	clockwise rotation	compressed rotation
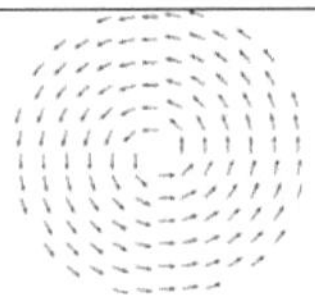	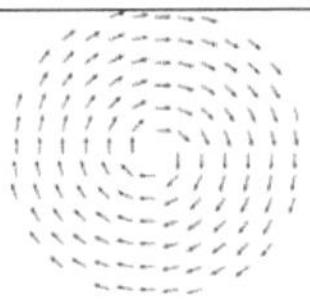	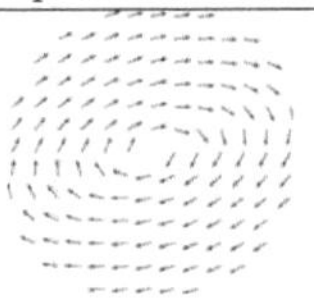
$\Psi_1 = i\frac{2}{3\sqrt{\pi}}$ $\Psi_{2,3,4,5} = 0$	$\Psi_1 = -i\frac{2}{3\sqrt{\pi}}$ $\Psi_{2,3,4,5} = 0$	$\Psi_1 \approx -i\,0.1677$ $\Psi_{2,3,4,5} = 0$
swirl	saddle	homogeneous flow
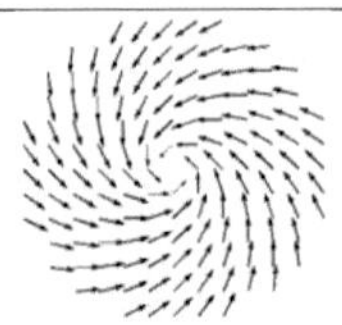	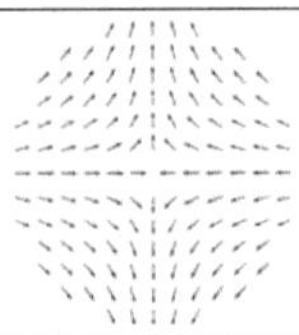	
$\Psi_1 = -\frac{2}{3\sqrt{2\pi}} + i\frac{2}{3\sqrt{2\pi}}$ $\Psi_{2,3,4,5} = 0$	$\Psi_1 = 0$ $\Psi_{2,3,4,5} = 0$	$\Psi_1 = 0$ $\Psi_{2,3,4,5} = 0$

Figure 5.4: Invariant moment values for prototypical flow features. The fact that all second-order moments ($\Psi_{2,3,4,5}$) are zero for linear vector fields enables an easy recognition of these features.

5.2 Critical Point Characteristics of Flow Moments

for $(p+q) \leq 2$ yielding

$$\begin{aligned} m_{01} &= -\tfrac{1}{3}\pi \quad & m_{10} &= i\tfrac{1}{3}\pi \\ m_{00} &= m_{02} = m_{11} = m_{20} = 0. \end{aligned} \quad (5.12)$$

Because the integration is performed over the unit circle (having area π) with the critical point as centroid, it yields $\eta_{pq} = \frac{1}{\pi\gamma} m_{pq}$, $\gamma = \frac{p+q+2}{2}$. Thus, equation (5.2) can be applied to calculate the moment invariants:

$$\begin{aligned} \Psi_1 &= i \tfrac{2}{3\sqrt{\pi}} \approx 0,376126389\, i \\ \Psi_2 &= \Psi_3 = \Psi_4 = \Psi_5 = 0. \end{aligned} \quad (5.13)$$

This calculation can also be performed for other critical features, i.e., clockwise rotation, convergence, divergence, or saddles. The calculation is performed in the same way. The results obtained for these critical features are illustrated in figure 5.4. Obviously, only the first-order invariant moment $\Psi_1 = c_{01}$ is non-zero for most of the observed features. Rotation patterns have a purely imaginary value in c_{01}, while it is real for convergence and divergence. This fact even holds for compressed versions offering a simple algorithmic way for a good classification of these features. Furthermore, turning each single vector belonging to a pattern 90° counter-clockwise yields a multiplication of c_{01} with the complex number i. Moreover, this fact holds for any kind of pattern:

Corollary 5.2.1 (Component-wise Rotation) *Turning each vector of a flow field f solely by 90° counter-clockwise results in the moments of this modified version $\tilde{f}$ being the moments of f multiplied by the imaginary number i: $\tilde{c}_{pq} = ic_{pq}$.*

Proof: Let $\tilde{f}$ be a version of f with equal domain rotated by 90° counter-clockwise, i.e. $\tilde{f}(x,y) = \begin{pmatrix} \tilde{f}_1(x,y) \\ \tilde{f}_2(x,y) \end{pmatrix} = \begin{pmatrix} -f_2(x,y) \\ f_1(x,y) \end{pmatrix} = f(x,y)$. Further let all moments of $\tilde{f}$ be denoted with a $\sim$. Then it holds

$$\tilde{m}_{pq} = \int_{-\infty}^{\infty} \int_{-\infty}^{\infty} x^p y^q \left(-f_2(x,y) + i f_1(x,y) \right) dx dy$$

$$= i \int_{-\infty}^{\infty} \int_{-\infty}^{\infty} x^p y^q \left(f_1(x,y) + i f_2(x,y) \right) dx dy$$

$$= i m_{pq}.$$

As η_{pq} is a linear combination of m_{jk} and as f and $\tilde{f}$ are defined on the same domain, the normalization factor is the same which implies

$$\tilde{\eta}_{pq} = i \eta_{pq}.$$

As c_{pq} is a linear combination of η_{jk}'s the assertion

$$\tilde{c}_{pq} = i c_{pq}$$

follows.

□

The continuous representation of purely homogeneous flow as well as saddles have their moment invariants being zero. This can be resolved by taking into account an already precomputed parameter: the absolute value of the sum over all vectors in the pattern $|m_{00}|$. For saddles $|m_{00}|$ vanishes, while it is definitely non-zero for a homogeneous flow. Instead of $|m_{00}|$ one can also use the shifted and scaled version $|c_{00}|$. In section 6.2 a method for highlighting critical features using the described properties is presented. Second-order moment invariants are relevant for more complex patterns, i.e. being important for the pattern recognition algorithm presented in chapter 6.

Taking a closer look at the values of c_{01} one can observe a relation to the Helmholtz-Hodge decomposition. For details of the Helmholtz-Hodge decomposition it is referred to [FP99]. Drawing the values of the flow patterns into a diagram reveals this connection. While rotational behavior of a pattern is mapped into the imaginary space, divergence and convergence is mapped into the real space. Figure 5.5 reveals furthermore that all patterns that can be constructed by combination of rotation and sink/source patterns are located on a circle in the complex graphical representation of c_{01}.

5.2 Critical Point Characteristics of Flow Moments

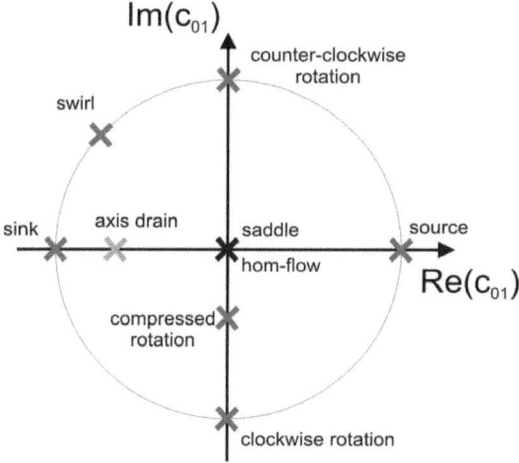

Figure 5.5: Graphical representation of $\Psi_1 = c_{01}$. Special critical points are marked by an "X". Images of all possible weighted combinations of rotation and sink/source patterns result in a circle with radius $\frac{2}{3\sqrt{\pi}}$. Saddles and homogeneous flows both map onto zero. Compressed versions of pure rotations or sinks/sources stay on the corresponding axis. This is also the case when modifying a sink to an axis drain feature. The fact that divergence and convergence only contribute to the real part of c_{01} and rotational behavior only contribute to its imaginary part shows the connection to a Helmholtz-Hodge decomposition.

Chapter 6

Algorithms for Fast Flow Pattern Recognition

Pattern recognition in flow fields differs from pattern recognition in images especially by the fact that the patterns in images are usually considered to be special objects. Segmentation and classification of these objects form a basis for easy object recognition. So, the understanding of a general pattern recognition in flows is very different from the one in image data. In flow data no sharp object borders can be observed. Only the topological behavior might be used for segmentation of flow fields, as for example done by Ebling and Scheuermann [ES06]. However, segmenting flow fields according to seperatrices is not equivalent to image segmentation. A comparison of flow features is even more difficult, regarding domain and values. Moreover, it limits the possible patterns again to the topological behavior of a flow. To provide a more general approach it is reasonable to consider all possible patterns for the recognition process. In the following section 6.1, it will be illustrated how the *multi-scale moment pyramid*, a special information basis, is constructed. Using this information basis two algorithms are derived. First, a method for the immediate recognition and visualization of critical points is presented in section 6.2. Second, and most important, a method for the general recognition of flow patterns given on a circular domain is illustrated in section 6.3. While both algorithms are able to process standard data-set sizes in real-time, the preprocessing cannot be done that efficiently, but equivalently efficient to the recognition of *one single pattern* using the former methods as described by Heiberg [HEWK03], Ebling and Scheuermann [ES03, ES05b], and Schlemmer [Sch04], illustrated in section 6.3.

6.1 Moment Pyramid

For developing fast algorithms for pattern recognition or for searching special features a data basis of pre-computed information is very helpful. Thus, the idea is to pre-compute the values for a flow field for various possible patterns and store them as a look-up-table. Having given this information, searching for a specific pattern in the flow field reduces to computing the moment invariants for this single pattern and comparing these values to the stored ones. The information data basis can in this case be built up as a so called moment pyramid. The following paragraphs explain how it is built and discusses further optimizations to enable high-speed pattern recognition.

Invariant moments are mainly used in image processing and font recognition. They are usually applied to a pre-segmented portion of a given data set. A vector field segmentation implies, however, strong restrictions to special regions of flow behavior. To keep the system general for the recognition of arbitrary flow patterns, the whole data set has to be taken into account. Thus, a multi-scale approach for analyzing 2D flow data has been developed, described in section 6.1.3. This approach can be used for an invariant pattern recognition. To extract the information of a data set at various scales, one has to use windowing functions to extract the information. For covering the whole field one can apply a correlation operation. Thus, the flow vector moments is discretized to filter masks and the correlation is performed by a convolution of mirrored masks with the field enhanced by a Fast Fourier Transform (FFT) implementation. The discretization and convolution process is described in detail in section 6.1.1.

The convolution is computed for all discrete radii resulting in the moment pyramid. Since the convolution operation increases continuity by one degree, small perturbations in the radii between these discrete positions tend to have only very limited effects. Since the convolution operator covers the whole field, translation invariance becomes obsolete for this special application of the theory. This does not mean it becomes obsolete in general, i.e., for the given settings the centroid has to be chosen to be located in the center of each filter mask.

In section 5.1.3 two types of scale invariance have been mentioned. Depending on the application one might be only interested in the directional behavior of vector patterns. If total scale-invariant moments are chosen, vector magnitude has a big influence on the results, i.e., patterns that are equal in directions and different in scale are not recognized. Therefore, it is reasonable to homogenize the vector length of the field and store the magnitude information separately as a scalar field. The direction information can be examined using flow vector moment invariants with domain scale invariance. Flow magnitude can be regarded as an image and be processed using the pyramid approach with the standard scalar moment invariants, as presented in section 2.3. If one is only interested in recognizing structures that are both, similar in vector direction and length, one has to change the computation from *domain scale invariance* to *total scale invariance*.

6.1.1 Correlation with Moment Filter Masks

For an efficient computation of the flow moment invariants of the complete field a correlation of the field with specific moment filter masks has been implemented in in the context of this work. In equation (5.2) it is shown how complex moments can be represented by normalized central moments. Those moments can be easily derived from regular moments m_{ij}. Regular moment filter masks can be discretized and computed independent from the data. It is the correlation of these masks with f that result in the moments m_{ij}. Figure 6.1 shows the basis functions $x^p y^q$ that are discretized to the moment masks.

For an efficient computation, the correlation is performed as a convolution with mirrored filter masks. The convolution can be enhanced by using component-wise Fast Fourier Transforms (FFT) and multiplication in frequency domain, as presented in section 2.2.2. The normalized central moments η_{ij} are calculated by application of shifting and scaling onto m_{ij}. As rotation invariance cannot be fully guaranteed for rectangular masks, the moments are trimmed to a circular isotropic domain around the chosen centroid. Those can be used to compute the complex moments c_{pq} (see equation (5.2)). Inserting these values into the invariant basis $\mathcal{B}_2$, one obtains according to equation (5.9) the values $\Psi_1, \ldots, \Psi_5$. These values are finally invariant to translation, scaling, and rotation for any kind of given pattern.

6.1 Moment Pyramid

Figure 6.1: Moment masks represented as continuous 2D functions.

6.1.2 Overcoming Discretization Issues

For small mask sizes the coarse discretization of the moment calculation introduces a high relative error. This is because the domain ought to be circular. Larger mask sizes are better in approximating this circle. So, the usage of super-sampling can strongly increase accuracy for smaller mask sizes. The heuristic applied is to use a five times super-sampled field for mask sizes from 5x5 to 20x20, and for all others the regular field size. This procedure lifts accuracy of a 5x5 moment computation to the stable 21x21 moment computation. The improvement in accuracy is also depicted in table 6.1. The fact that an improvement can be reached by super-sampling, as well as the fact that the developed theoretical foundations are based on continuous data also show that this new method is also applicable on arbitrary grids or pure point set data without an underlying grid (see also section 6.1.4).

6.1.3 Multi-scale Moment Pyramid

For each scale of the filter masks correlations are performed, each resulting in a field on a two-dimensional domain containing the invariant moments $\Psi_1, \ldots, \Psi_5$. Those fields become smaller for increasing scale of the filter masks, since the border region is left out. Thus, the resulting collection of moment fields is called *moment pyramid*.

A moment pyramid provides a discretized description of all possible vector patterns of an underlying field, stored with height corresponding to the scale of the pattern and the corresponding position at each specific scale level of the pyramid.

The complete construction process of a moment pyramid is illustrated in figure 6.2.

6.1.4 Generalization

Although the implementation concentrates on circular features, there are ways to handle differently shaped patterns. Patterns can be subdivided into (overlapping) circular regions. Those regions can be analyzed or used as input for a search algorithm. A search algorithm regarding these connected regions has to be extended with a method that compares the positions of each circular pattern finding, enabling a classification of non-circular patterns. Although, global features, like for example separatrices cannot be found directly with this method one might specify pattern regions that are characterizing separatrices. Moment invariants can be be utilized for vector field segmentation also resulting in separatrices in future work.

Another point that has already been mentioned is the extension to unstructured grids. This can be done in an elegant fashion, as the theory of vector moment invariants is formulated for continuous data. Though, to achieve this there is a need for a new data structure, as the presented moment pyramid has been designed for uniformly structured data. Another possibility would be to keep the data structure for this purpose and just use the super-sampling method at very high resolution for unstructured grid data. Of course, in this case a good interpolation method is essential for good results. An additional uncertainty visualization should also be

6.1 Moment Pyramid

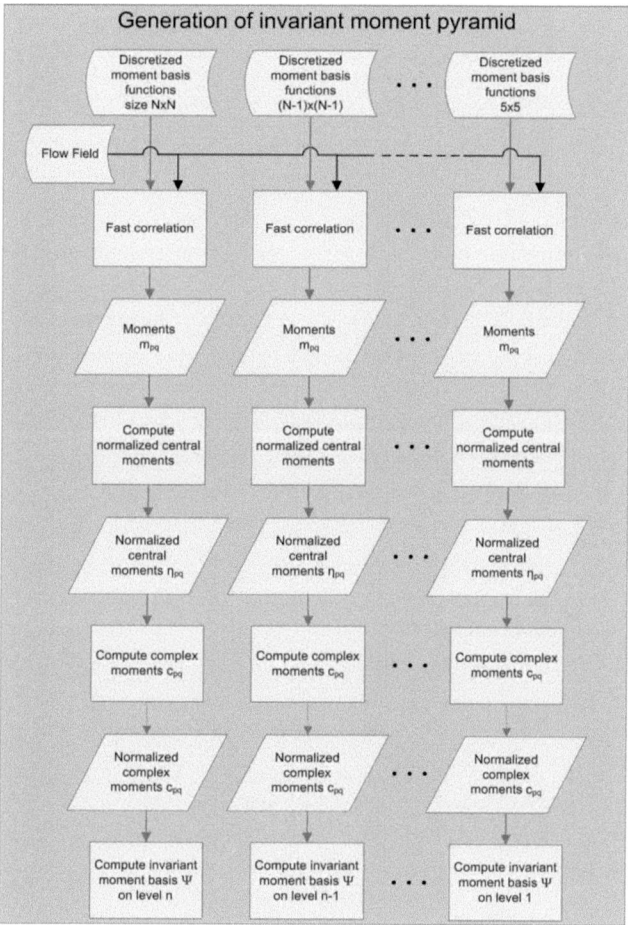

Figure 6.2: Construction of a moment pyramid. First, regular moments m_{pq} are computed by correlation of the field with given basis functions. Second, translation and scaling transforms m_{pq} to normalized central moments η_{pq}. The alternative complex representation for these normalized central moments η_{pq} are the complex normalized central moments c_{pq} derived by equation (5.2). Finally, one can compute the flow moment invariants $\Psi_{1,...,5}$. This process is done for all possible discrete pattern sizes starting with 5x5, resulting in a pyramid structure.

included in this case, depending on the density of the input samples. This can also be an aspect of future development.

6.2 Critical point recognition and visualization

As shown in section 5.2, invariant moments have certain properties for critical point features. This work proposes an algorithm for highlighting 2D critical point features, i.e., rotations, sinks, sources. Saddles need further inspection, as first and second-order moment invariants are zero, equally to any homogeneous flow pattern. This can be solved as explained in section 5.2 by observing the value of $|m_{00}|$ or $|c_{00}|$.

The algorithm uses a preprocessing step to compute a sorted list of pyramid positions. The positions are sorted according to a combination of the absolute values of the second-order moments $\Psi_{2,3,4,5}$, i.e., sorted according to a parameter $n = |\Psi_2| + |\Psi_3| + |\Psi_4| + |\Psi_5|$. The resulting list has the critical features, as well as homogeneous flow patterns, at its front end. Excluding all feature values with the first-order value Ψ_1 near or equal to zero, results in a list that is sorted according to criticality. Processing this list is straightforward: the list is traversed to a user-defined point. Each entry contains the pyramid position that maps directly to position and scale in the field, enabling a fast visualization. The method is used to highlight rotations in a Boussinesq flow data set (see figure 6.3).

Operating on discretized features results in approximations of the continuous values. Discretization results and deviations are presented in table 6.1 exemplarily for the rotation pattern observed in section 5.2. As one can see, the super-sampling approach for small scales strongly helps improving the results obtained with the moment invariants.

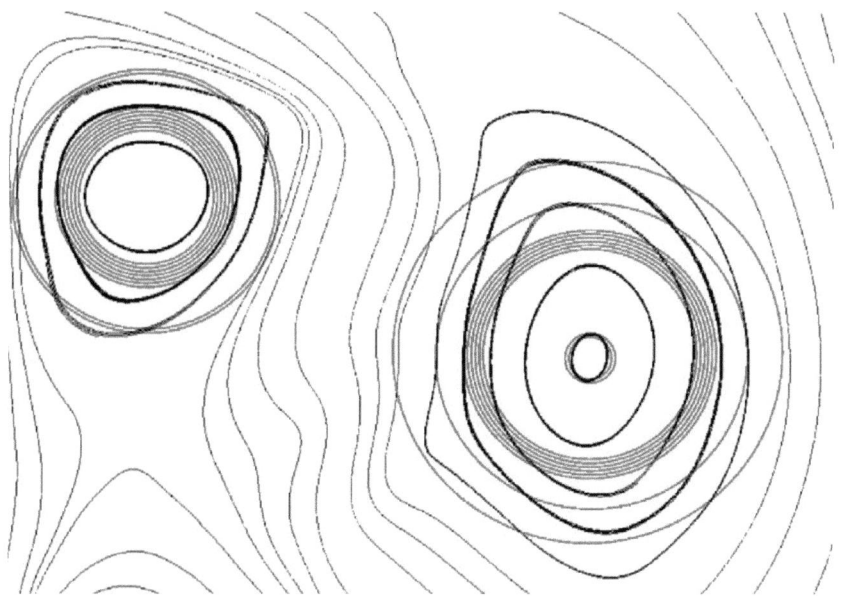

Figure 6.3: Rotations in a Boussinesq flow (see section A.1). Features found by searching with the criticality index highlighted by red colored circular region markers.

6.3 Fast Pattern Recognition in Flow Fields

Besides the recognition of critical points, moment invariants can be used for the fast recognition and classification of arbitrary features. In the context of this work, a fast pattern recognition for 2D flow vector data using the theory of flow moment invariants has been developed. In a preprocessing step a moment pyramid is computed for the given data. This pyramid stores the complex moment invariants $\Psi_1 \ldots \Psi_5$ for local regions of the field. Further, a sorted offset of the moment values of Ψ_1 is computed, linking to the positions in the pyramid. The choice of Ψ_1 is reasonable,

resolution	$\mathrm{Im}(\Psi_1)$	absolute deviation	relative deviation [%]
5×5	0.408543	0.032417	8.6187
$5 \times 5^*$	0.380274	0.004148	1.1028
10×10	0.386398	0.010272	2.7311
$10 \times 10^*$	0.376822	0.000695	0.1849
25×25	0.373890	0.002236	0.5945
50×50	0.379709	0.003582	0.9524
75×75	0.376525	0.000398	0.1059
100×100	0.376557	0.000430	0.1144
200×200	0.376339	0.000213	0.0567
continuous	0.376126	-	-

Table 6.1: Results of the discrete moment computations compared with the continuous value of a counter-clockwise rotation feature (*using the super-sampling approach). Super-sampling improves accuracy. Values converge faster for odd pattern sizes. For proper recognition of exact patterns the relative deviation parameter δ should be chosen by assuming worst case deviation of the calculation, i.e., to capture small scales $\delta \approx 1\%$, and higher for the recognition of similar patterns.

as it is a first-order component containing the major part of the information. Therefore, the pattern matching algorithm can be performed very efficiently. A pattern is selected, the computation of the invariant moments for a single pattern is done rapidly, a delta region around the computed offset reveals a short list of similar pattern candidates, which can be compared in the remaining moment invariants $\Psi_2 \ldots \Psi_5$.

Since arbitrarily defined patterns can be recognized invariant to scale and rotation, no time-intensive additional convolutions are necessary during execution time. Similar patterns can be highlighted almost in real-time. The only drawback of this method, the high usage of memory, could be overcome by storing only the first component in the pyramid. This would save disk space, but on the other hand lead to a little higher latency, as moments must be computed for all matches. Since the complete moment pyramid is also used for other applications, it is reasonable to perform the pattern recognition with the larger version. More ideas on how the moment pyramid size can be reduced can be found in the future work section in chapter 9.

6.3 Fast Pattern Recognition in Flow Fields

S-shaped pattern	Diverging pattern
$\Psi_1 = 9.804 \cdot 10^{-03} - i \cdot 2.294 \cdot 10^{-01}$	$\Psi_1 = 1.064 \cdot 10^{-01} + i \cdot 8.634 \cdot 10^{-03}$
$\Psi_2 = -2.294 \cdot 10^{-01} - i \cdot 8.264 \cdot 10^{-03}$	$\Psi_2 = 1.581 \cdot 10^{-02} + i \cdot 1.543 \cdot 10^{-03}$
$\Psi_3 = -1.888 \cdot 10^{-03} + i \cdot 1.187 \cdot 10^{-03}$	$\Psi_3 = 2.445 \cdot 10^{-03} + i \cdot 2.285 \cdot 10^{-04}$
$\Psi_4 = -1.894 \cdot 10^{-04} + i \cdot 5.633 \cdot 10^{-06}$	$\Psi_4 = -3.709 \cdot 10^{-05} - i \cdot 4.484 \cdot 10^{-06}$
$\Psi_5 = -2.226 \cdot 10^{-07} - i \cdot 1.540 \cdot 10^{-06}$	$\Psi_5 = -2.367 \cdot 10^{-09} - i \cdot 6.079 \cdot 10^{-09}$

Table 6.2: Moment invariants for two example search patterns. An S-shaped structure from the swirling jet data set (see figure 6.4) and a diverging structure in the Boussinesq flow data (see figure 6.5).

In contrast to other algorithms for pattern recognition in vector fields (like Ebling and Scheuermann [ES03] or Heiberg [HEWK03]), the presented algorithm is able to detect any kind of pattern without an extra computation of rotated or scaled versions. To illustrate this, two examples for extra-ordinary pattern searches, showing that the patterns do not have to satisfy any special properties are discussed. Figure 6.4 shows the swirling jet data set discussed in section A.5, the pattern, and the matches. The moment invariants for the search pattern can be found in table 6.2. Each pattern has been detected correctly. Note that there might be other S-shaped structures not being found because of their different directional behavior not being depicted in the streamline representation. This can be tackled by comparison of the magnitude of real and imaginary part in the first-order component Ψ_1 separately so that the sign is skipped.

The Boussinesq flow, explained in section A.1, is shown in figure 6.5. A detection of a specific diverging flow pattern has been performed yielding in good results. By increasing the relative deviation δ, the search space is increased. This takes effect on computation time, but increases the number of matches.

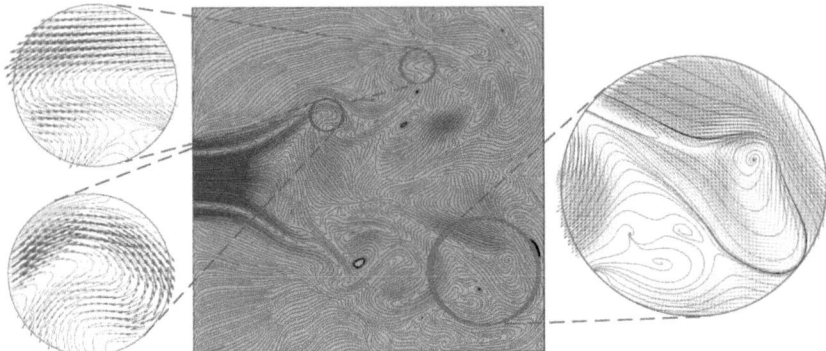

Figure 6.4: Swirling jet flow (section A.5). An S-shaped pattern is searched for and found three times at different scales for $\delta = 0.7$. General data visualized with streamlines, close-ups of the matching structures including hedgehog representation. Even though the swirls in the right image distract the viewers attention the global S-shaped structure has been recognized. Underlying color map and colors of the hedgehog representation of the zoomed versions display the velocity of the swirling jet data. [SHM+07]

These algorithms have been integrated into the *CoVE (Comparative Visualization Environment)* system (implementation by Morr [Mor07]) enabling a parallel pattern search in multiple data sets. Patterns can be specified by selection, by definition (through an integrated pattern editor), or by browsing through invariant moment space. The identified patterns are then highlighted in all visualized data sets, allowing a comparison in a highly effective way complex flow data sets based on arbitrary flow features.

Comparing the algorithm to the algorithms of Heiberg [HEWK03], and Ebling and Scheuermann [ES03], the herein presented preprocessing step for all searches is approximately as expensive as the other methods to search for one single pattern. The result of this preprocessing, however, makes it possible to search for all kinds of patterns in almost real-time, even for larger data sets. In the following, it is explained why the presented preprocessing step and the search times of the mentioned methods are similar.

6.3 Fast Pattern Recognition in Flow Fields

While for the other algorithms, many rotated versions for any scale of the pattern have to be correlated with the chosen field, for the presented method a correlation with ten predefined basis functions m_{ij} is performed. This correlation step is the most expensive (but still highly optimized) part and has to be performed for all methods. For the presented method, the results have to be sorted and stored as a search data basis, while the other methods do not need to do this. The other methods have to compute the rotated and scaled versions prior to the correlation and they have to combine the search results for the rotated and scaled versions to a final similarity map. All in all the presented preprocessing step and the mentioned algorithms got approximately the same complexity.

Having the preprocessing step done once, multiple freely definable patterns can be searched for each in almost real-time. This is far better than the computation time for one single pattern using the other algorithms. The only disadvantage of the new method is that these patterns have to be defined on a circular domain. This issue can be overcome by an advanced search approach as discussed in section 6.1.4. Quantitative results for the preprocessing step, the calculation of the moment pyramid and for the search operations are illustrated in figure 6.6. Results have been computed on a Athlon X2 4600+ with 2GB RAM. The point where search times suddenly increase can be explained by the fact that for larger data sets the search in the moment pyramid has to be performed on the hard disk and not in the main memory. The higher the deviation is chosen, the less similar become the result patterns. If one would like to find somewhat similar patterns, he or she can enter a higher deviation. This is computationally more expensive as more possible results have to be compared with the actual moment values. A smaller deviation is a more strict criterion and yields less result positions, meaning less computation time.

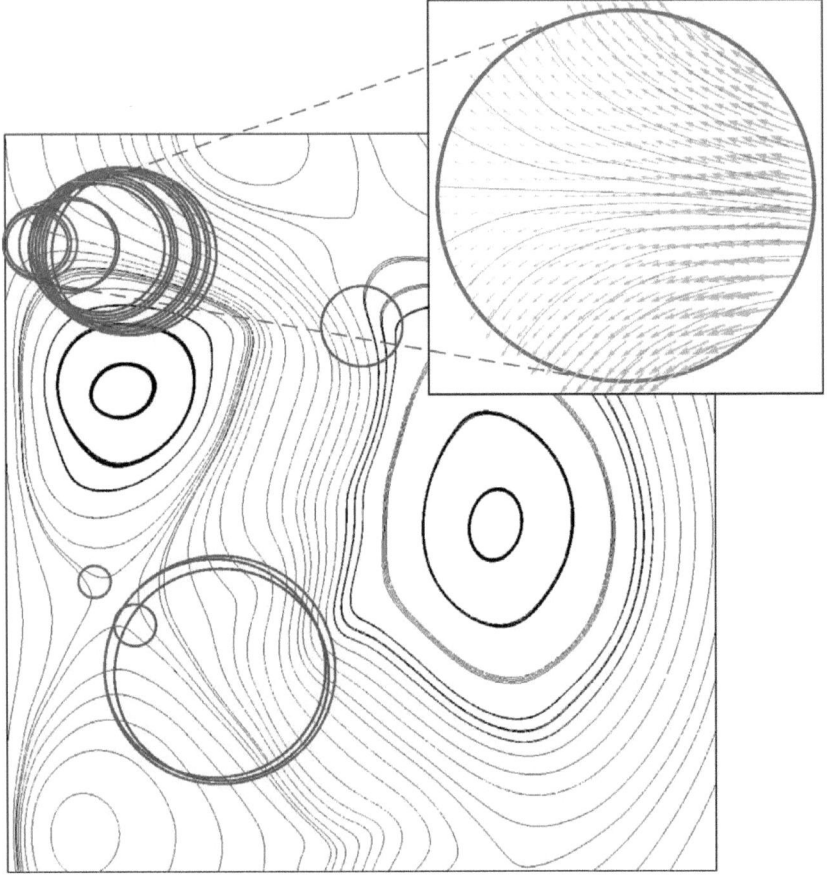

Figure 6.5: Search results for a specific pattern in the Boussinesq flow with $\delta = 0.5$. A zoomed representation of the original pattern is given in the upper right corner. [SHM+07]

6.3 Fast Pattern Recognition in Flow Fields

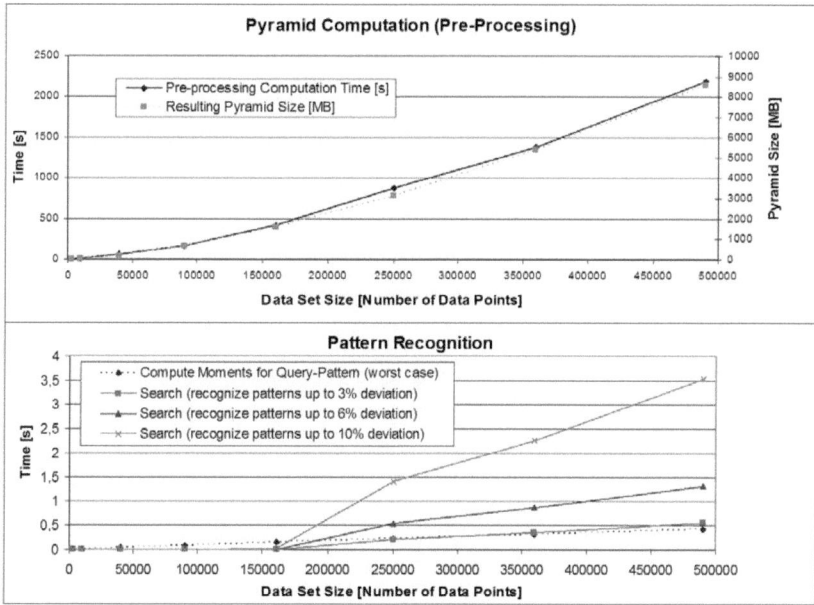

Figure 6.6: Computation results for scaled versions of the Boussinesq data set. The upper diagram shows information on the preprocessing step for generating the moment pyramid. The lower diagram shows the recognition times for arbitrary circular patterns. A sudden time increase at a data set size of 500x500 can be observed for the reason that for larger data sets the pyramid exceeds the main memory. Search times still remain acceptable. [SHM+07]

Part IV

Context-based and Comparative Flow Visualization

Chapter 7

Priority Streamlines

In context of the visualization pipeline, the previous chapters have mainly been dedicated to the filtering process, namely the recognition of scalar and flow features. In this chapter, however, a novel visualization technique for an improved highlighting of these recognized flow features is presented. The idea is to use the resulting similarity fields or regions of pattern occurrences as context information for a context-sensitive streamline approach. In this context a general context-sensitive streamline drawing approach has been developed.

The goal of the proposed method is to draw streamlines in 2D and 3D space, being based on a user-given context, and highlighting important features by higher rendering density. Unimportant information shall not be shown in the final visualization. The work incorporates some ideas of Salisbury et al. [SWHS97] who use orientable textures and a special importance definition to render line drawing images. Color and transparency can be used for displaying more information on the highlighted streamlines. The user will be enabled to define certain priorities for regions or patterns. Thus, the streamlines are called *priority streamlines* [SHH$^+$07]. However, the final image may not look very "pleasant" (e.g., by disregarding the uniformity criterion); instead the goal is to produce an informative and revealing visualization.

There are for example, some methods that can control streamline density globally (e.g. Turk and Banks [TB96], as well as Mebarki et al. [MAD05]). These methods are described in section 2.1.3. Here is a typical application example of the idea of *priority streamlines*: a geologist researching a magma flow might be interested in seeing streamlines mainly in regions where a high temperature gradient occurs. Of course, one can use Mattausch's approach and draw evenly spaced streamlines with color mapping. However, this will result in occlusion. Moreover, one loses the freedom of using color mapping for other purposes, as another data dimension could be illustrated through the use of colors (for example, the viscosity of the material). All yet known methods (see 2.1.3 place an emphasis on seeding. Another important issue, the usage of different streamline densities, is sometimes mentioned, see Mebarki et al. [MAD05], but the regions always have to be chosen manually by the user. In addition it is not used for visualizing further attributes of the data.

7.1 Definition of the Streamline Density

The first point to take care of is the definition of streamline density. A streamline with a finite, non-zero line width and length covers a certain area when it is drawn.

Definition 7.1.1 (*Global Streamline Density*)
*Given a domain Ω and a set of streamline regions $R_S \subseteq \Omega$, the **global streamline density** D_g is defined as:*
$$D_g = \frac{\int_\Omega \chi_{R_S} d\Omega}{\int_\Omega 1 d\Omega},$$
where $\chi_{R_S}(x) = \begin{cases} 1 & , \text{ if } x \in R_S \\ 0 & , \text{ if } x \notin R_S \end{cases}$ *is the characteristic function of the subset $R_S \subseteq P$.*

It is reasonable to use a discrete representation, since in practice streamlines are drawn on a grid with certain resolution.

7.1 Definition of the Streamline Density

Definition 7.1.2 *(Discrete Global Streamline Density)*
*Let the domain P be a set of pixels and the subset of streamline pixels $S \subseteq P$. The **discrete global streamline density** D_{dg} is defined as:*

$$D_{dg} = \frac{\sum_{p \in P} \chi_S(p)}{|P|},$$

where $\chi_S(x_i) = \begin{cases} 1 & , \text{ if } x_i \in S \\ 0 & , \text{ if } x_i \notin S \end{cases}$ *is the characteristic function of the subset $S \subseteq P$ and $|P|$ the total number of pixels ($i \in \{0, ..., |P|-1\}$).*

This definition is quite instructive, since the number of occupied pixels divided by the total number of pixels indicates, in a range of $[0, 1]$, how dense the streamlines are.

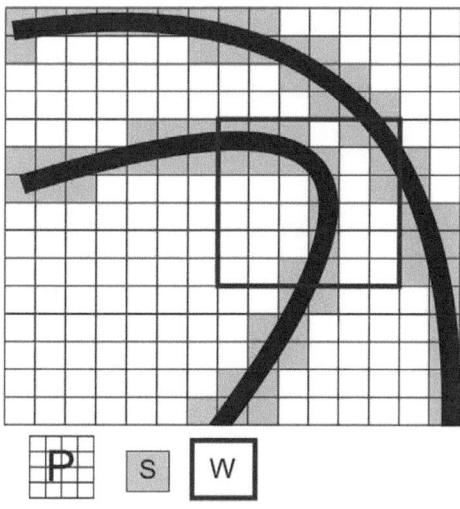

Figure 7.1: Discrete streamline density definition. The definition of density is based on the ratio of counted streamline pixels to the total number of pixels on the whole domain P or on a local domain W.

Another interesting characteristic is the local streamline density. A certain density can be achieved by local windowing over the domain.

Definition 7.1.3 (Discrete Local Streamline Density) *The discrete **local streamline density** D_{ld} for a window $W \subset P$ is given as:*

$$D_{ld}^W = \frac{\sum\limits_{p \in W} \chi_S(p)}{|W|}.$$

Figure 7.1 illustrates the streamline density definition.

7.2 Priority Streamline Algorithm

7.2.1 General Idea

For the streamline generation a so-called *density map* is constructed. According to this map streamline start points are seeded (mainly depending on the maxima of the map). The generation of each streamline lowers the density map locally until the map's global maximum is below a certain threshold. If this threshold is reached, the final image is ready. The algorithm will terminate in any case, as the density map is strictly monotonic decreasing over time. Figure 7.2 illustrates the algorithm generally as a flow diagram. The following paragraphs of section 7.2 will explain the basic algorithm with more details. Two major issues, the density map and the filtering, are further inspected in sections 7.3 and 7.4.

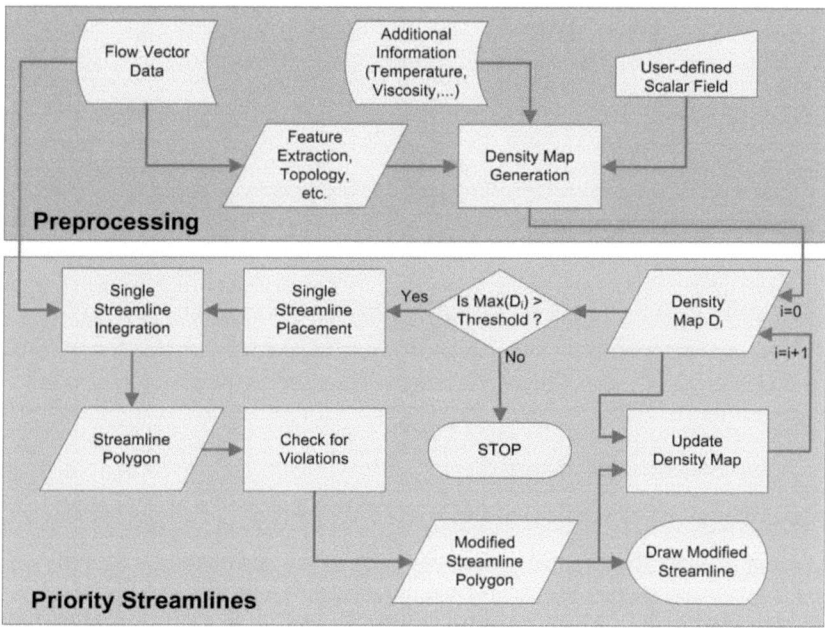

Figure 7.2: Flow diagram of priority streamline algorithm.

7.2.2 Density Map

Given a flow vector data set, streamlines with a certain density varying density should be drawn. This density is given by a scalar function defined on the domain of the flow vector data set. This *density map* can be derived in many ways:

- *Definition considering additional data dimensions:*
  Application scientists often have more information than pure vector data. Temperature, viscosity, density, color, granularity, etc. could also be taken into account and define this map.

- *Definition considering derived vector information:*
  Given a vector field, one can calculate, for example, velocity and vorticity, with no additional information needed for their computation. The topology of the field could be computed and serve as basis for the density map. Another way of deriving it from the field might consider pattern recognition algorithms, see section 3. Of course, the presented efficient pattern matching algorithm using moment invariants (chapter 6) can be also be used as density map.

- *Definition by user:*
  Regions of interest can be defined user-driven by drawing the 2D or 3D density function manually. Moreover, the user can use pre-defined density maps and further edit them.

During the execution of the algorithm, the *streamline density map* is updated after each single streamline calculation, having an effect on further seeding positions as well as stop criteria. The construction of the *density map* is discussed in section 7.3.

7.2.3 Streamline Seeding

For the seeding of streamlines, seeding points can be placed directly at the current point of interest. This point is defined by the current streamline density map. For the first streamline, this is the maximum value of the initial density map. However, there is a special case, where this concept fails. If assuming a constant density map, start points would be picked in a row. To prevent this, a small amount of noise is added to the *initial density map*, not influencing a non-uniform distribution.

7.2 Priority Streamline Algorithm

The random noise values are chosen to be much smaller than the field values, so that the resulting seeding positions do not change noticeably, but for the case of a totally uniform distribution. As the map is updated after each step to prevent too-close seeding, the next maximum is chosen to seed the next streamline. In order to fulfill the continuity criterion, the algorithm computes the distances of the next five maximum positions to the last streamline start point and takes the farthest of these as current maximum. Another option would be to fully apply the farthest streamline seeding of Mebarki et al. [MAD05]. However, the five-maximum strategy turned out to be working well, too.

7.2.4 Calculation of the Streamlines

Given the streamline start position a full streamline is integrated in both directions. The general idea is to subtract a blurred, rasterized version of the streamline from the corresponding values of the *density map*. This can be done basically in two ways:

1. One can draw the streamline into a binary image, convolve it with a Gauss-like filter and subtract this image from the given density map.

2. One can traverse the streamline and subtract a Gauss-like filter kernel at each position consecutively from the density map.

The first method can be enhanced by calculating the convolution in frequency domain by using the fast Fourier transform (see section 2.2.2.2). This would lead to a complexity of $O(n\, log_2(n))$, with $n = |P|$ being the total number of map pixels/voxels. This is in general too high a cost when processing 3D data. The second method, referred to as *traversal algorithm*, turned out to be much more efficient. It is visiting every point of the streamlines and performs a filtering. As the filter size is fixed, the resulting computation complexity is linear, i.e., it is in $O(m)$, with the number $m = |S|$ of streamline pixels/voxels being much smaller than the total number $n = |P|$ of pixels/voxels. For this reason, this method is more suitable to apply the filter function.

In detail, the polygon vertices of the streamline are mapped into the corresponding discrete density map space. There, from the start point, the Bresenham line drawing algorithm, see [Bre65], is applied to each of the polygon segments in both integration directions, to find the centers of the filter for each step. The Bresenham algorithm is a fast and robust algorithm for addressing each pixel/voxel of this mapped streamline.

The update process is split into two phases:

1. Checking for a violation

2. Final update of density map and drawing of streamline

In the first phase, the traversal algorithm checks whether a violation of the density map occurs when drawing the streamline. If the subtraction of the filter function results in negative values at any place of the map, the traversal algorithm stops and the last valid streamline pixel/voxel is stored (for both directions). At this point, both streamline ends have been located. In phase two, the possibly shortened streamline is drawn on the screen and the map is updated by a second application of the traversal algorithm.

7.3 Construction of the Density Map

For the construction of the *density map* a scalar field is defined in the domain of the flow vector field. This scalar field can be given by additional data, user-defined, extracted as derived information from the vector field, or a combination of these (section 7.2.2).

In the first step, the scalar function f is discretized onto a fine regular grid, the so-called map. The resolution used for this discretization can be chosen according to the desired minimal streamline distance. This minimal streamlines distance can be increased by choosing a higher resolution.

The density map is required to be non-negative. Depending on the application, this can be achieved in three ways: by computing the absolute value, by shifting, or by setting the negative values to zero.

Since a specific class of filters is applied (see section 7.4 for details), the *density map* has to be scaled to obtain appropriate results. The choice of the scale factor determines the general density of the drawn streamlines. The minimum height of the density function is defined to have value 1.0. The maximum value of the function is user-defined and determines the *streamline goal density*, as well as the *degree of importance*.

Definition 7.3.1 *(Initial Density Map)* Let $[a, b]$ be the *range interval of the input scalar function*, $a, b \in \mathbb{R}$. The goal range interval of the density map is defined as $[1, c]$, with $c \in \mathbb{R}$ being the so-called **importance factor**. The linear map $f : [a, b] \to [1, c]$ with

$$f(x) = \begin{cases} \frac{(x-a)(c-1)}{b-a} + 1, & \text{if } a \neq b \\ 1, & \text{if } a = b \end{cases}$$

is defined to be the **initial density map** or interchangeably the **streamline goal density**.

The importance factor c can be selected by the user. If the factor is chosen near 1.0, the distribution of the streamlines is rather homogeneous. Increasing it yields an increasingly heterogeneous distribution according to the underlying importance map.

7.4 Filtering

Section 7.2.2 mentioned that the density map is lowered frequently by a Gauss-like filter. The Gaussian filter kernel has been chosen for the reason that it is isotropic in all dimensions and allows us to produce a smooth transition between focused parts and edge regions. In addition, the filter needs to incorporate a minimum distance. No streamline should lie in a certain ϵ-region next to another streamline, to avoid clutter. One approach to solve this problem is to define a second map, where those regions are marked separately. This can also be done in a simpler, more efficient way by using a trick in the filter design. The idea is to modify the Gauss filter that is the basis of the proposed filter. The major difference is the center region. There, a large negative value (ideally $-\infty$) is set. When the filter is subtracted from the map, the result is a very high value in the map (ideally ∞). For further streamline seeding points of value higher than c are excluded. Thus, no streamline is placed in the *forbidden regions*. Moreover, an additional check in the *violation checking traversal algorithm* is added. If there is a higher value than c at the current position, it lies in a forbidden ϵ-region and the streamline is stopped. With these additional steps the *minimal streamline distance* is defined and controlled.

Another difference to the Gauss filter is its maximum value and its overall sum. Usually, a Gauss function is normalized to have integral value 1. In contrast to that, the used filter is defined to have value 1 as maximum, not considering the integral. Of course, with a global definition one could control the number of streamlines by choosing a global scaling using a *density map* with a given volume and subtracting the Gauss filter volume frequently along the streamlines. But this turns out to be very complicated. For example, it is necessary to estimate the final streamline length in advance. Therefore, the simpler local approach for the definition of the *density map* and the filter have been chosen. To have a common basis, the maximum

7.4 Filtering

value of the Gauss-like filter is defined to be 1. Figure 7.3 shows a representation of the constructed filter. The final filtering process is also illustrated for a function in Figure 7.4.

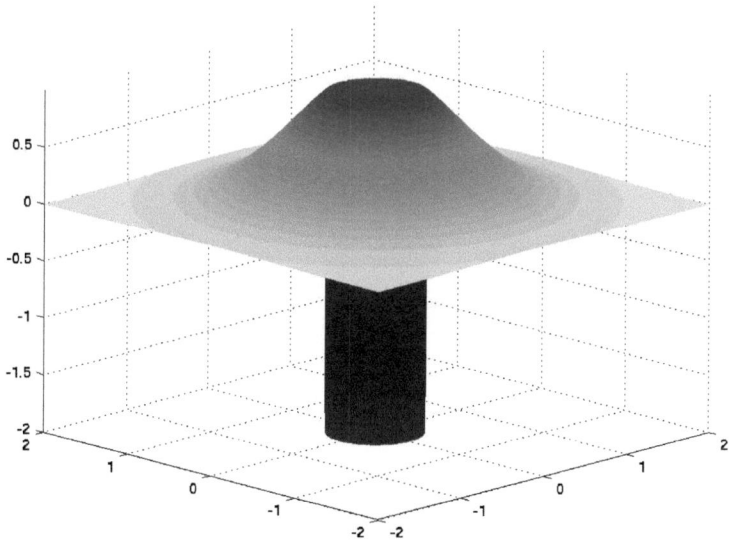

Figure 7.3: Constructed Gauss-like filter for 2D-data. The center region is set to a large negative value.

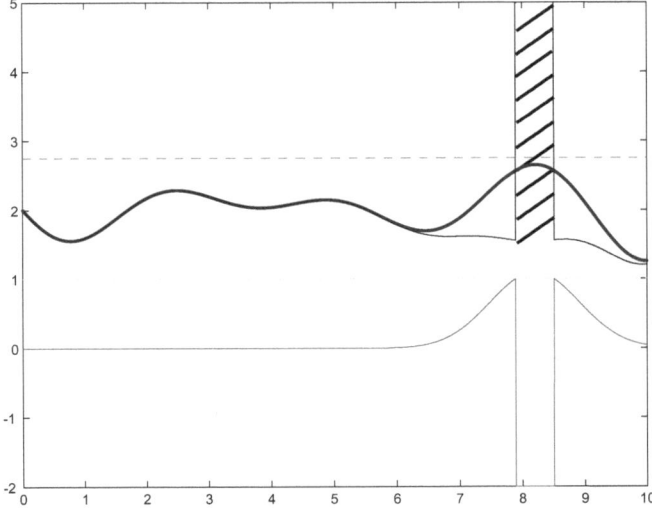

Figure 7.4: Filtering process illustrated for 1D-case. The density function is at its global maximum (below the dotted line) subtracted by the filter. The resulting function acts as density function for the next iteration. The hatched area shows the minimal distance zone of a streamline, where further placement is forbidden. The process is repeated until the global maximum of the current density function also lies below a certain threshold.

7.5 Results

To demonstrate the results, *priority streamlines* have been applied to numerically simulated data as well as simple synthetic data for test purposes. The method has been tested for 2D and 3D data. The implementation was done in Python and embedded into the visualization tool *CoVE, Comparative Visualization Environment* [Mor07]. The results have been generated on an Intel Centrino M 1.5 GHz, 512 MB RAM notebook.

First, artificial vector fields are discussed, see Figure 7.5. They consists of 512x512 vectors and represent two saddles, one sink and one source respective four saddles. For these vector fields three different *density maps* have been used. The first one was chosen completely homogeneously to compare the algorithm with standard algorithms. The second one was chosen to have a high-valued center region and zeros on the edges, to show that the algorithm can be used for windowing purposes as well as for representing features through change of streamline density. The third density map highlights the saddle points. The algorithm has been applied by using various parameters. Adjusting the resolution of the density map and filter size directly affects overall streamline density. In section 7.3, the so-called importance factor c has been explained. By increasing this factor, the influence of the underlying density is increased and a higher degree of heterogeneity (depending on the given density map) is introduced, see Figure 7.5(b).

As an example for non-trivial 2D data a simulated data set representing a swirling jet entering a fluid at rest has been used (see section A.5). The data is given on a rectilinear, non-uniform grid. Figures 7.6(a) and (b) show the data imaged with standard streamline generators, compared to images generated using the velocity field of the data as *density map*. One can see that the standard streamlines do not provide any information on velocity, while the new approach reveals the velocity through streamline density. Other visual mappings like color mapping can be used to visualize and compare other properties of the data. This property will enable a kind of *comparative visualization*, being discussed in section 8.1.

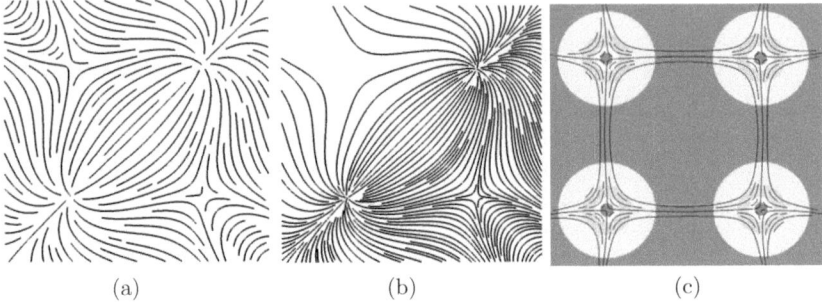

(a) (b) (c)

Figure 7.5: Two test datasets: (a) and (b) two saddles, one source and one sink, (c) four saddles and one center point. (a) Streamlines drawn by the priority streamline algorithm using (a) a constant density map, (b) a heterogeneous density map: values of density map increase from the upper left to the lower right corner. (c) a density map highlighting saddle points. The density map is shown as background color.

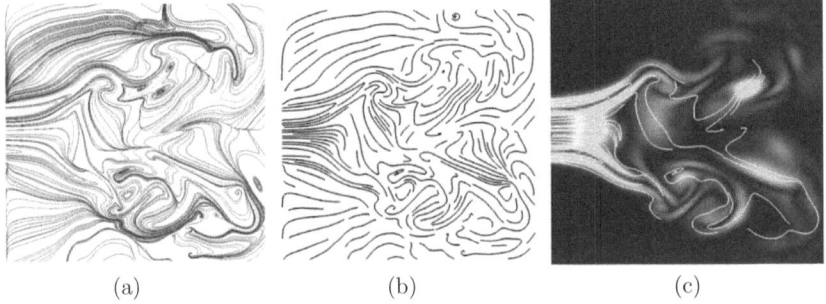

(a) (b) (c)

Figure 7.6: (a) Swirling jet entering fluid at rest. Visualized with standard streamlines. (b)Swirling jet data visualized with priority streamlines using velocity magnitude as density map. (c) Swirling jet data visualized with coarser priority streamlines and additional velocity color mapping.

7.6 Conclusions

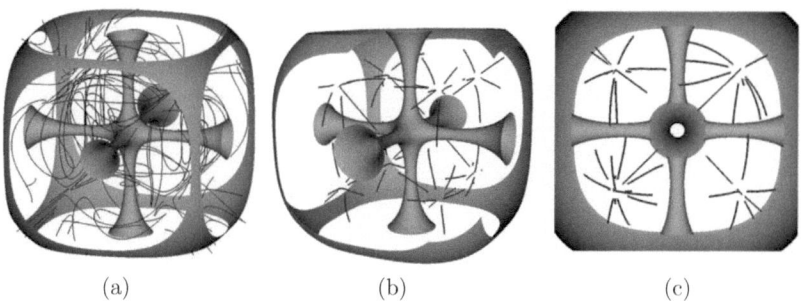

(a)   (b)   (c)

Figure 7.7: A velocity isosurface has been visualized to give a visual reference for all images. (a) Eight saddles test data visualized with standard streamlines. (b) Eight saddles test data visualized with priority streamlines, sloped camera position. (c) Eight saddles test data visualized with priority streamlines, camera view along an axis.

Finally, the algorithm has been applied to 3D data. An artificial test data set is shown in figure 7.7. It contains eight saddles. While streamlines computed with a common random seeding algorithm fail to capture these features, *priority streamlines* are able to give an idea on how flow behaves especially in these regions. If an additional feature should be visualized, this can for example be done by adding *priority streamlines* in a different color. This will be discussed in more detail in the context of *comparative visualization*, where the method is applied to 3D simulation data sets in section 8.1.

7.6 Conclusions

In this chapter, a new algorithm for drawing streamlines with a defined heterogeneous density has been presented. It is useful for various tasks. *Priority streamlines* can be used to present additional properties beyond vector data (like temperature), to represent implicitly given but not visualized data (e.g., velocity, vorticity, etc.), to compare or to filter (e.g., to reduce clutter in 3D visualizations). Priority streamlines can also be used to compute homogeneously distributed streamlines. The results for homogeneous distributions are not as good, as those obtained with special solution approaches, focusing on homogeneity. The algorithm should not be seen in competition with these techniques, as the goals of *priority streamlines* are different. The *continuity* criterion is neglected to obtain a higher degree of freedom for the representation of different streamline densities and filtering purposes. The implementation is designed efficiently using a preprocessing step to decrease computation time during user interaction. The results show that the user is enabled to control the visualization in ways to highlight and extract certain information. Control parameters can be chosen manually or be derived automatically.

Chapter 8

Comparative Visualization

While the previous chapters have been dedicated to *feature-based visualization* approaches, this chapter gives ideas on how the presented techniques can be used for *comparative visualization*. Foundations and notes on previous work in this area can be found in section 2.1.4. First, the possibilities of using *priority streamlines* for feature comparisons will be illustrated. The second idea is to use the interactive pattern matching on flow data (as presented in chapter 6.3) to provide comparative data control to the user. However, the comparison can also be done not only on specific patterns, but by the analysis of the moment feature space. Comparing feature spaces of neighboring time steps of time variant data does again result in a comparative visualization.

8.1 Comparative Streamline Visualization

The *Priority Streamlines* as presented in chapter 7 can also be used to visualize features comparatively. This can be used in two or three dimensions. For two dimensions, one can for example draw streamlines for one feature and a color map for a second feature. The streamline color has to be chosen to have a high contrast to the color mapping space to get best visual results. As an example, Figure 8.1 shows the *priority-on-high-velocity* streamlines together with a scalar color mapping representing vorticity. One can see that there is a relation between vorticity and velocity. In regions of high vorticity there is lower velocity. As this is a known fact, it confirms

Figure 8.1: Comparative visualization of velocity (streamline density) and vorticity of swirling jet data.

8.1 Comparative Streamline Visualization 127

the validity of the method. Other visualization parameters like transparency, illumination, varying streamline thickness (streamtube thickness), etc. could be used for mapping additional properties. A second idea is to visualize certain features of a flow field with streamlines of a certain color. By doing this, it is possible to display a large variety of data dimensions in context of a two- or three-dimensional scientific visualization. The aim of this visualization technique is comparable to parts of the *SimVis*-project from Doleisch et al. [DGH03]. While SimVis is focusing on displaying colored particles by suitable brushing, *Priority Streamlines* represent an alternative approach in a similar direction. An advantage of the SimVis approach is the integrated data brushing technique. Though, data brushing is not implemented yet for *Priority Streamlines*, there is the advantage of an additional integrated flow representation. The brushing approach can be included similarly to the pattern recognition approach. The brushing as well as the recognition result yield in a scalar map, being the input for drawing priority streamlines.

There are of course still issues with the three dimensional representation of streamlines. Using advanced streamline techniques, like illuminated streamlines, this issue can be overcome in most cases.

All in all, the colored streamlines give a good impression of the compared features. To give examples, a flow vector data set from a simulation of convection in the Earth mantle has been visualized using *priority streamlines*. The density map has been chosen in a way that the method acts as a filter and represents only streamlines in desired regions. The desired regions can be chosen manually (through editing the 3D density map) or by mapping any other property of the data to the density map. The example visualization considers density maps based on velocity, temperature and different criteria for vortex region detection: vorticity and Okubo-Weiss parameter. The latter parameter can be used to decompose a potential vorticity field into three different fields, as defined in [PJW06]: vortex cores (high vorticity areas), strain/circulation cells (region with high shear surrounding vortex cores), and background (remaining vorticity after cores and strain cells are removed). The Okubo-Weiss (OW) parameter is a relation between vorticity $\omega \in \mathbb{R}$ and strain $S \in \mathbb{R}$:

$$OW = S^2 - \omega^2.$$

Within a vortex core, the vorticity dominates, meaning $OW < 0$ Dominating strain is indicated by $OW > 0$. Details can be found in the original formulation by Okubo [Oku70], at Petersen et al. [PJW06], and at Sahner et al. [SWH05].

Figure 8.2 shows all streamline types using different colors. One can see the basic flow behavior as well as other important properties (e.g., vorticity , velocity, and temperature distribution) in just one image. Clutter, a major issue in visualizing streamlines in three dimensions, is reduced by our algorithm. The second example is a snapshot of the velocity field of a 3D mixing layer. Figure 8.3 shows three different views onto the result generated by our method using various density maps together with an vorticity isosurface. The representation of scalar fields using streamline density makes is possible to display several fields at a time without occluding each other. This allows a side by side comparison of these fields, e.g., two different parameters for vortex detection (direct computation of vorticity compared to the Okubo-Weiss negatives). Figure 8.2 shows a convection simulation, a magma circulation in the earth mantle. Obviously, the temperature is higher at lower levels, so these streamlines give an impression of the flow behavior in this region. The lines in the middle are indicating high velocity. In this core region the magma transfer to the surface is strongest. The Okubo Weiss positives indicate high strain regions. Obviously, the strongest region is the region of highest velocity. The Okubo Weiss negatives are indicating the vortex core lines, such as the streamlines generated from the vorticity density map (two vorticity regions spread like two wings from the center).

Figure 8.3 shows a numerical simulation of turbulences. The image was again generated using *Priority Streamlines*. Three parameters are shown: Okubo Weiss negatives and vorticity again indicate vortices, while Okubo Weiss positives indicate strain.

To conclude, these images display the basic principle of the comparative visualization with *Priority Streamlines*. Drawing these streamlines with additional illumination will further enhance the three dimensional impression. Even though, the images give an insight into the capabilities of the method, being suitable for displaying many additional data dimensions together with flow information in just one visualization.

8.1 Comparative Streamline Visualization

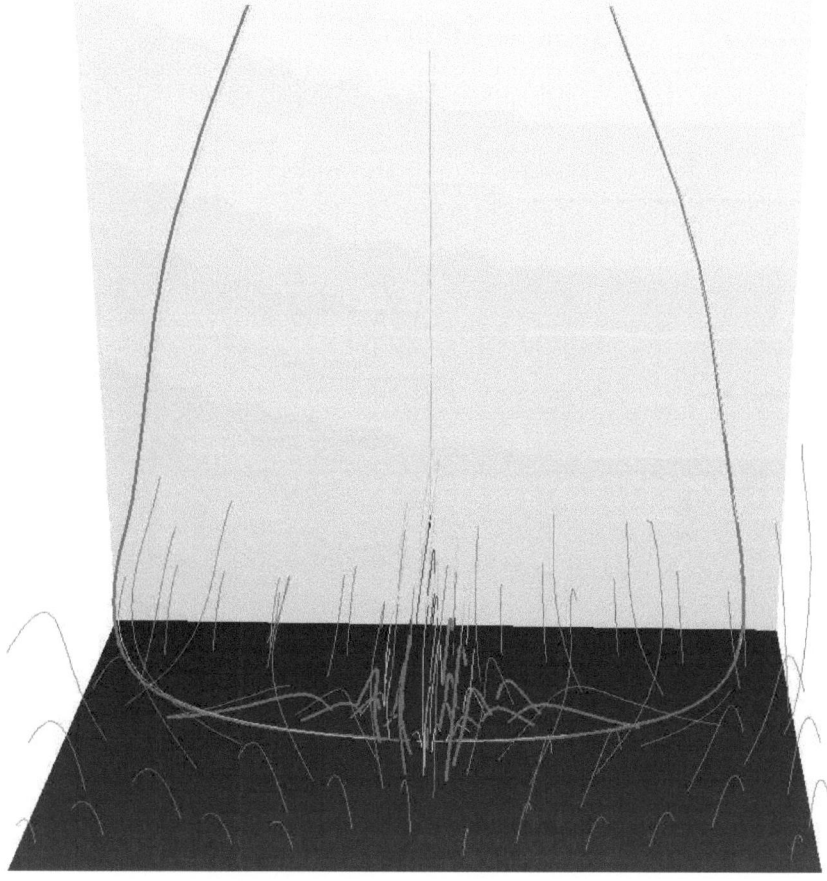

Figure 8.2: Convection in Earth mantle. Variously colored streamlines indicate high vorticity, high velocity, negative OW values, positive OW values, high temperature level.

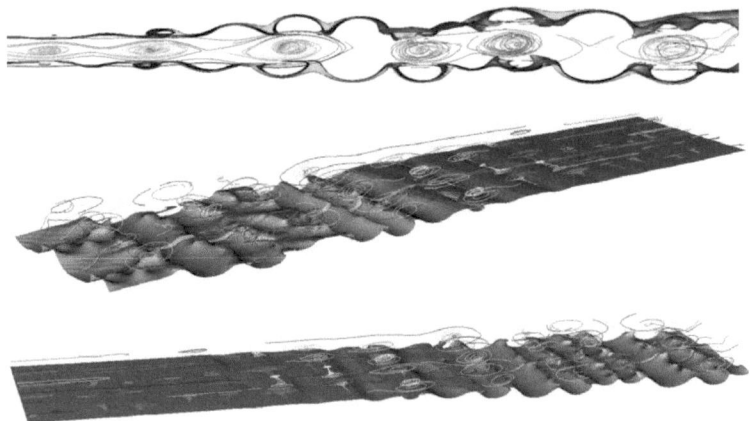

Figure 8.3: Snapshot of the velocity field of a 3D mixing layer. Three views onto the dataset. Red: streamlines indicate high vorticity, yellow: high velocity, green: (strongly) negative values for OW, blue (strongly) positive values for OW. The colored version can be found in our publication [SHH+07].

8.2 Interactive Pattern Comparison

In this section an approach for a *side-by-side comparative visualization* is presented. The idea is to show visualizations of two or more data sets next to each other and use the fast pattern recognition for an interactive highlighting of similar features. This works for scalar and all kinds of vector data (images and flows), since the pattern recognition method can be applied on both kinds of data (using the common flow moment invariants for scalar/image data and the *flow moment invariants*, chapter 5, for flow data). Nevertheless, the main goal of this dissertation is the analysis of flow data. In the following, three flow data sets are visualized using the *interactive pattern comparison*. The Boussinesq flow simulation (see section A.1) is compared to the swirling jet flow simulation (see A.5), and a flow simulation of Hurricane Isabel, an Atlantic cyclone that appeared at the American east-coast in September 2003 (see A.2).

8.2 Interactive Pattern Comparison

Figure 8.4 shows the software *ComPARE - Comparative Pattern Analysis in a Realtime Environment* that has been especially designed for this purpose. The idea is to keep visualization efforts low to enable an interactive pattern recognition. So, the main part of the visualization was done with *CoVE - Comparative Visualization Environment*, the rendered image (color-map and streamlines) was saved as an image. *ComPARE* computes the moment invariants of a field in a pre-processing step using FFTW [FJ07]. As described in section 6.3, the time for this computation is about the same time than computing one single pattern search with previous methods. After this pre-computation all pattern searches can be performed interactively. The pattern is chosen from the data underlying the *selection image* on the left, the search results are indicated on the right with circles (or plus signs, alternatively). The colors of the circles indicate the degree of similarity. Furthermore, in the middle, the tolerance can be adjusted.

Another important point to mention is that the moment field is a discrete representation of an at least $\mathbb{C}^1$-continuous field. This is due to the fact that it has been obtained by the *convolution operator*. So, it is natural to find many similar values in a specific region. However, visualizing all results yields clutter, as there are certain areas, where values are similar in the direct neighborhood. Thus, if results are in the direct neighborhood of each other, only the more similar result will be visualized. This increases the clarity of the visualization. Finally, the moment representation of the current search pattern is shown in the upper-middle of the screen. This setting has been used for the recognition of three test patterns.

Comparative Visualization

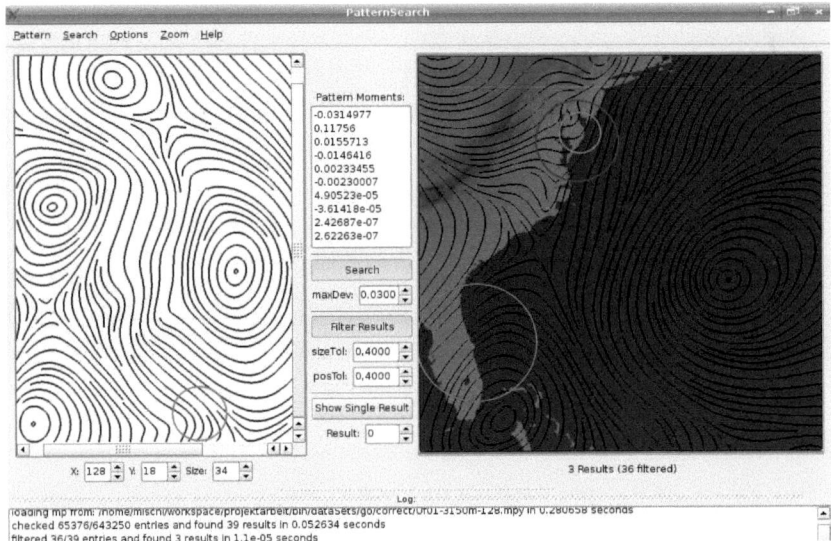

Figure 8.4: Screenshot of the *ComPARE* - visualization software. A typical comparative pattern search is shown for the Boussinesq flow (selection field, left) and a time step of the Hurricane Isabel data set (search field, right). The visual representation was generated by *CoVE* and loaded as a pixel map. The visualization of the patterns is done by colored circles. Moment values, deviation and filter controls are located in the center. A pattern recognition on the flow data can be triggered and performed interactively by using simple mouse operations in the left window. The response time is less than 0.4 seconds for data sets ≤ 200000 data points.

8.2 Interactive Pattern Comparison

Figure 8.5: Interactive pattern recognition in multiple flow fields: Hurricane Isabel data (upper left), Boussinesq flow (upper right), and swirling jet (lower left) are compared visualizing the occurrence of a selected test pattern. Similarity to the original moment values (lower right) are indicated by the colors of the circles: highest similarity up to 3% relative deviation.

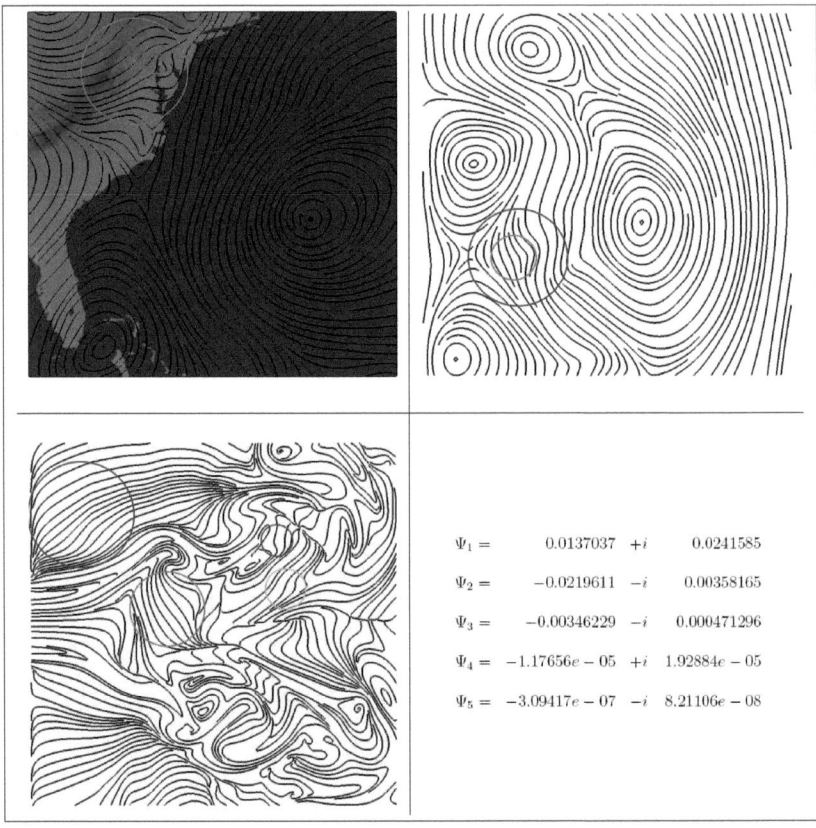

Figure 8.6: Interactive pattern recognition in multiple flow fields: Hurricane Isabel data (upper left), Boussinesq flow (upper right), and swirling jet (lower left) are compared visualizing the occurrence of a selected test pattern. Similarity to the original moment values (lower right) are indicated by the colors of the circles: highest similarity up to 3% relative deviation.

8.2 Interactive Pattern Comparison

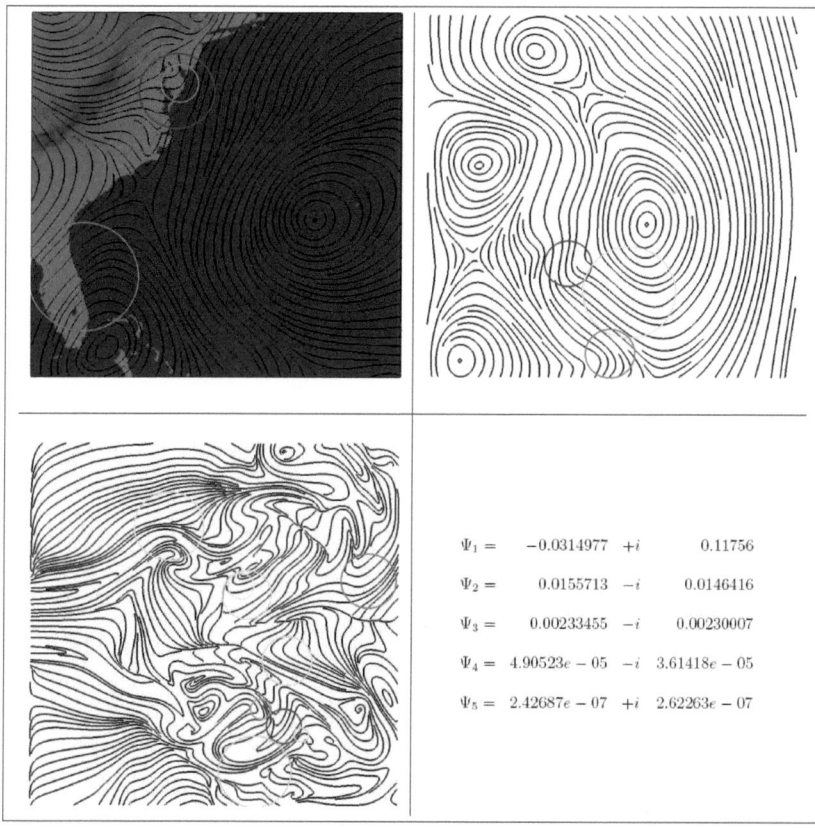

Figure 8.7: Interactive pattern recognition in multiple flow fields: Hurricane Isabel data (upper left), Boussinesq flow (upper right), and swirling jet (lower left) are compared visualizing the occurrence of a selected test pattern. Similarity to the original moment values (lower right) are indicated by the colors of the circles: highest similarity up to 3% relative deviation.

8.3 Comparative Visualization of Time-Variant Data

In this section, two methods for the analysis of time-varying flow data are being presented. The comparison is based on features, especially on spatial flow structures. However, there is no focus on special structures (like sources, sinks saddles, etc.) but on the observed general flow behavior. Information regarding the flow structure in differently sized circular areas is stored in a feature vector: the flow moment invariants (see Chapter 5.1.1). To cover the whole field the feature vectors are stored in a so-called moment pyramid (as explained in section 6.1).

The definition of a suitable metric for the comparison of moment invariants is a key element.

8.3.1 Difference Metrics

For all subsequent definitions let the flow moment invariant for a pattern P be given by $\Psi^P_{1,...,5}$ and for a second pattern Q by $\Psi^Q_{1,...,5}$. P and Q shall be compared.

Definition 8.3.1 The **first order absolute distance** d_1 of the two patterns P and Q is defined as
$$d_1 = \left|\Psi^Q_1 - \Psi^P_1\right|.$$
The **second order absolute distance** d_2 is defined as
$$d_2 = \sum_{i=2}^{5} \left|\Psi^Q_i - \Psi^P_i\right|.$$
The **complete absolute distance** d_c is defined as
$$d_c = d_1 + d_2 = \sum_{i=1}^{5} \left|\Psi^Q_i - \Psi^P_i\right|.$$

The absolute distances are defined according to the common distance metric of complex numbers. For the second order moment invariants the sum of all second order distances is computed. The complete absolute distance is a combination of

8.3 Comparative Visualization of Time-Variant Data 137

the first and second order. The terms might also be normalized, but there is no need to normalize. In the following, a definition for a relative deviation is given.

Definition 8.3.2 *The **complete relative deviation** δ of the two patterns is defined as*

$$\delta = \max\left(\left\{i \in \{1,...,5\} \left|\frac{2|\Psi_i^Q - \Psi_i^P|}{|\Psi_i^Q| + |\Psi_i^P|}\right.\right\}\right).$$

Using this metric, changes in pattern structure can be observed relatively. This formula unfortunately becomes singular when comparing two completely homogeneous structures or perfect saddles, yielding zero in the denominator. One might also obtain a good relative deviation measure with only one element in the denominator (like $\Psi_i^P|$). However, this choice leads more often to singularities. Furthermore, the comparison operation would not be commutative. For this reason the denominator has been chosen as presented in 8.3.2.

Both metrics indicate the similarity of the underlying structures. The lower the distance (deviation) is, the higher is the similarity of the two compared patterns. The highest degree of similarity is obtained for patterns with equal moment invariants having zero distance (and deviation).

8.3.2 Interactive Pattern Comparison

In this section an approach for a *feature-based data comparison* is presented. The idea is to generate visualizations of multiple data sets next to each other and use the pattern recognition to highlight similar features. This can be especially useful for the comparative visualization of neighboring time steps from time-dependent flow data. A pattern of interest is chosen by the user by selecting an arbitrary circular region in the spatial domain of a specific time step. The moment pyramid is addressed using the mentioned index. For the comparison of the query pattern moment invariants with the elements in the pyramid, the complete relative deviation metric is used. The desired maximum deviation is chosen by the user, for example $\delta = 3\%$. This means that positions in the moment pyramid where all moment value components $\Psi_{1,...,5}$ vary up to 3% from the moment components of the pattern of interest are marked. The position in the moment pyramid directly maps to the position and scale in the original field, meaning the pattern recognition returns all positions and corresponding scales of similar flow structures of any time step of the time-varying data. Another important point to mention is that the moment field is a discrete representation of an at least $\mathbb{C}^1$-continuous field. This is due to the fact that it has been obtained by the convolution operator. It is natural to find many similar values in a specific region. However, visualizing all results yields clutter, as there are certain areas where values are similar in the direct neighborhood. Thus, when results are in the immediate spatial neighborhood of each other, only the most similar result are visualized. This increases the clarity of the visualization. For this reason, a neigborhood of 1/4 -radius (a heuristic that can be adjusted as desired) of the recognized pattern has been excluded.

To illustrate how the presented methods work in practice, the flow data set from Hurricane Isabel, generated in 2003, has been chosen. The pattern comparison was performed for a 2D layer at a height of 3150m, for the first five hours of the data set, before the hurricane hits the continent. The size of each field (one per time-step) is 500x500, each pre-computation took about 13 minutes (Athlon X2 4600+ with 2GB RAM), and the size of the moment pyramids are 3.1 GB, each. The user driven (interactive) pattern recognition took for the chosen deviation of $\delta = 3\%$ a maximum of 0.26 seconds for any of the shown search requests.

The pattern comparison method can, for example, be used to track patterns over time. To illustrate the results exemplarily, Figure 8.8 shows three different patterns being tracked over five time steps each. The relative deviation was chosen as $\delta = 3\%$ for all pattern searches. The first pattern shown on the left side is a mostly homogenuous flow diverging at one side. In the first time step, the pattern appears once between the two circulations and the saddle point. In time step two, the pattern changed its position towards the vanishing saddle. It is still similar enough to be tracked within the 3% similarity tolerance. Time step three shows the tracked pattern in light-gray, indicating that the pattern has changed its shape being almost outside the similarity tolerance. However, a new pattern of this kind is developing again at a position close to the position in the first time step. This pattern remains until time step five (the last analyzed time step). During the final time step, more patterns of this kind can be observed in the vicinity of the large hurricane turbulence. A pattern that has left the chosen similarity tolerance (devi-

8.3 Comparative Visualization of Time-Variant Data   139

ation) will not be high-lighted, even though the streamlines are looking somewhat similar. In such a case, there is the possibility to increase this value. However, if the tolerance is chosen too high, the visualization might become cluttered due to the increased number of results.

The second pattern tracked over the same time steps is a saddle (see Figure 8.8 in the middle). In this case, no other similar structures can be observed, as the additional saddle emerging in time step five is not in the similarity tolerance (3% relative deviation) of the tracked pattern. It is interesting to observe that this pattern remains mainly at the same position close to the coast. It becomes a somewhat larger in time step two, but reduces its size again in the following steps.

The third pattern (Figure 8.8 on the right side) indicated a perfect example why this method is more revealing than a pure visualization with streamlines. The pattern is also quite homogeneous, with a divergence on one side (towards the coast). It is moving somewhat, but is present in the northern coast region in all five time steps. The pattern is also detected in time steps four and five. In time step four, one would not have succeeded in finding this pattern, as the streamlines do not fully reveal it due to its reduced size. Again, no other similar pattern is appearing.

No false positives have been observed during all experiments.

8.3.3 Moment Pyramid Comparison

The idea of the *flow moment comparison* is similar to the *pyramid comparison* for image data. The *moment pyramid* spans a scale space, similar to the *Gauss pyramid* known from image processing. Subtracting a second pyramid element-wise from the original one yields a *difference pyramid*. For the comparison the metrics defined above are used: the first order, the second order, and the complete absolute distance as well as the complete relative distance.

The distances d_1, d_2, and d_c are calculated for each element of two given moment pyramids. One obtains a scalar-valued difference pyramid for each applied metric.

Figure 8.8: Interactive pattern recognition for the first five hours of a flow simulation (Hurricane Isabel at 3150 meters height): three patterns are selected from a slice at an early time step. The patterns, which stay similar, can be tracked over time.

8.3 Comparative Visualization of Time-Variant Data

The visualization of the values of a certain pyramid level indicates the similarity of two flow vector fields with respect to structures of a certain size. This means a low pyramid level indicates changes of small structures (high-frequency changes), while a higher pyramid level indicates changes in large structures (low-frequency changes).

In the following the pyramid comparison is shown for three different metrics: the complete distance, the first order distance and the second order distance (see Figure 8.9). Again, the flow data set from Hurricane Isabel, generated in 2003, has been chosen for this demonstration (a description can be found in Section 8.3.2).

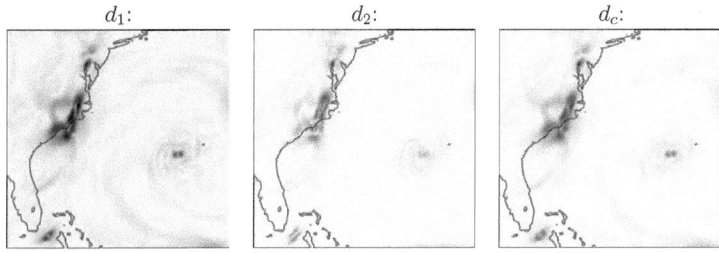

Figure 8.9: Moment pyramid (level one) comparison between the first and second time step of the Hurricane Isabel data (3150m height) for three different distance definitions.

The distance values are visualizing the movement of topologically and structurally important features. The movement of the saddle (see Figure 8.8 on the left side) can be seen clearly in this visualization, for first order, second order and combined moment distances. The movement of the center regions can also be observed. More examples for this visualization are presented in Figure 8.10.

For these visualizations, different pyramid levels have been analyzed. The total pyramid size is 120 layers for the presented data. Layer 60 is a medium layer. The moment distance at this level indicates changes of a medium or low frequency. The distances at such a level might be of value to analyze the future development of the storm. For example, the time step distance $3 - 4$ shows that two major regions of

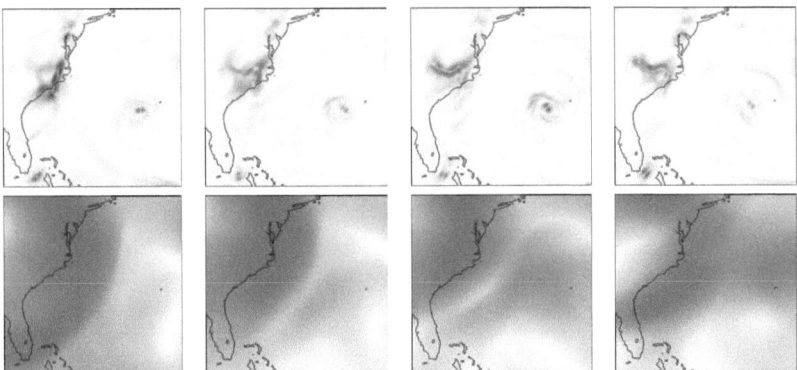

Figure 8.10: Moment pyramid comparison for different time steps of Hurricane Isabel. Distances on level one (high-frequency changes) are visualized in the upper row for similarity-distances between the time steps 1-2, 2-3, 3-4, and 4-5. In the row below, a higher level (half the pyramid's height) distance is visualized for the same time steps (indicating low-frequency changes).

activity are about to join. The resulting increased intensity can be observed along the coast at time step distance 4 − 5.

However, the high-frequency representation (meaning the visualization of the low pyramid-level distance) is revealing the movement and development of critical point features. Figure 8.11 shows the difference between step one and step five, meaning the changes over five hours. It can be observed that the small center south of Florida is slowly moving towards the coast. The large center, previously south-west of the Bermuda Islands has moved a little in north-western direction and is located west of Bermuda after five hours. The movement of the saddle point also shows an interesting pattern, first along the coast, then moving west. To conclude this Chapter, three methods for structure-based comparative visualization of 2D flow fields have been presented. Our first method applies *priority streamlines* as defined in Chapter 7 for a comparative flow visualization. The second approach uses an interactive pattern comparison based on flow moment invariants (as defined in Chapter 5) to observe the evolution of certain flow patterns over time. It has been demonstrated that this method can be used to track the flow patterns and observed movement, changes in

8.3 Comparative Visualization of Time-Variant Data

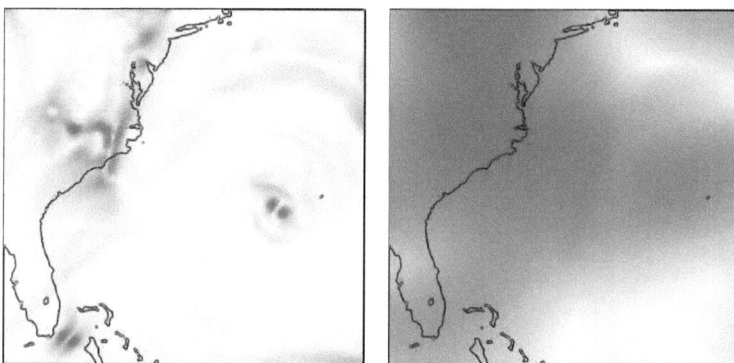

Figure 8.11: Moment pyramid comparison with distance between time step one and time step five for the first pyramid level (left) and the medium pyramid level (right).

size and orientation. The third contribution is the generation of difference images of the moment invariant space. This has been done for two levels of the flow moment pyramid to observe different scale frequencies. Different metrics have been presented to reduce the multi-dimensional complex-valued data. One metric has been studied in detail and it has been shown how this representation can be used to track critical flow behavior over time.

Chapter 9

Conclusions

The final chapter is assigned to conclude the ideas and algorithms. A new mathematical description of moment invariants for flow data, a fast flow pattern recognition method, and a novel approach for comparative flow visualization, both based upon this mathematical formulation, have been presented. Moreover, a context sensitive visualization method, the *Priority streamlines* were explained. This method is a valuable supplement comparative visualization possibility. Following up the state-of-the-art development, a method for color edge detection using the Clifford algebra has been presented.

Part one of the dissertation is a résumé of basic previous work and the state-of-the-art. In section 3.4 some open questions have been discussed. These questions have been addressed in the course of this work.

The main goal of this work was the visualization of flow data. The Clifford Fourier Transform by Ebling and Scheuermann [ES05b] was extended to non-uniform grids in [SHN+05]. This enables a fast pattern recognition of flow data for special features. However, the main issue of this method is that generally formulated patterns cannot be recognized at high speed. The pattern is searched for in a special size and orientation. So, for the recognition of a general non-symmetric flow pattern, the pattern has to be looked-up in all possible sizes and for all of these sizes in a large variety of discretized rotated versions. This turns out to be very time consuming, being far away from a method that should be called interactive (for this task). So, the idea was to find a method for the *interactive* detection of those general patterns. *Interactivity* is a very controversial term. The problem with it is that the term itself does not induce usability. One could also use the term *real-time*. But this term is also not a good description, since the time limit for so-called *real-time* application is up to the developer. The idea of *interactivity* in this work is that the application enables the user to directly observe results from a given input in an equitable time. In this context some few seconds might be acceptable, similar to the response times of the work with a web browser. For longer response times, the system might also be called *interactive* by definition, but not from the understanding of *interactivity* in this work.

The idea for a really interactive and usable method for flow pattern recognition came from the area of image processing. As mentioned, the main issue of the Clifford based methods was the changing orientation and scaling of the patterns. In image processing, shape descriptors like *moment invariants* are used to describe scalar patterns regardless from translation, scale, and orientation. However, the original descriptors can not be used for flow data. The main problem was that the direction of the flow is not considered by the image moment invariants. For this reason, the basis functions of these invariants have been reformulated in this work to perform on flow data. Further, it has been proven that it is really a basis, meaning that no irrelevant calculations have to be performed and the generated data is (in this context) minimal.

The idea for a interactive pattern recognition is to compute the moment invariants for all (or a large variety) of possible spatial patterns in a flow field in the course of a pre-computation. The pre-computation takes about as long as the recognition of *one* general pattern with the Clifford pattern matching method. During this pre-computation an ordered look-up-table (LUT) of moment value parts is generated pointing to the occurrences in the so-called *moment pyramid*. The moment pyramid is a simple extension of the field storing the moment values (bottom-up) for increasing pattern sizes. With this representation the visualization can be performed at high speed. After a search pattern is selected, the flow moment values of this pattern are computed, entered into the LUT, possible positions and scales are returned. The complete moment values for this fractional amount of positions are compared to the moment invariants of the search pattern. Those positions containing similar patterns in a certain user-defined tolerance are highlighted in the visualization.

The moment invariants have been analyzed, revealing certain interesting aspects, e.g. the fact that for first order critical points the second order moment invariants have turned out to be zero. This provides an alternative critical point detection and visualization method for two dimensional flow data.

Besides this main contribution, other interesting results have been obtained. As mentioned, the *Clifford color image edge detection* has been formulated. It turned out to be a different mathematical formulation of the common color image edge detection. However, the Clifford algebra is a suitable framework for this task and reveals some coherences between edges in the chrominance part of an image an flow fields. The presented work has shown that Clifford FFT and Clifford convolution can be used for the detection of edges in color images.

The last part of this work is dedicated to the visualization aspect. While the previous parts have addressed mainly the filtering process in context of the visualization pipeline, this part is dedicated to the generation of images. First, a novel streamline technique has been presented: the *Priority streamlines*. This technique can be used for the visualization of many additional data dimensions in the context of two- or three dimensional flow data. The idea is to compute streamlines with a pre-defined density. This density is generated from additional information, such as vorticity, velocity, pressure, temperature, pattern-guided, or user-defined.

Priority streamlines as well as *flow moment invariants* can be used to define new *comparative visualization* approaches. Chapter 8 presents three different methods for comparative visualization. The first one is the application of the *Priority streamlines* method for the comparison of different flow features in the context of a two- and three dimensional flow visualization. A parallel application of the interactive pattern recognition on multiple flow data sets leads to a second comparative flow visualization method. Finally, the time steps of time-variant flow data sets can be compared by the same method and in addition by a *moment pyramid comparison*. This comparison can also be used for the identification and tracking of critical point features in the flow.

Future developments should include the development of a valid three dimensional moment invariant basis. The used moment invariants are defined on complex numbers. A proper extension is provided by quaternions, as well as the three dimensional Clifford algebra. However, this yields an at least four dimensional domain. An idea to overcome this issue is a projection into the three dimensional space by the application of unity quaternions. However, this does not suffice, since only the three-dimensional imaginary part is kept. As there is no hyper-complex algebra for three dimensions, it is more promising to try to derive the flow moment invariants for three dimensions from a non-complex formulation of the image moment invariants in combination with a suitable three dimensional basis like spherical harmonics.

The flow moment invariant fields are multi-dimensional fields with a degree of at least $\mathcal{C}_1$ continuity in each dimension. This information can be highly valuable for data reduction purposes with methods developed in the area of *geometric modeling*, also being a task for future work.

To conclude, a mathematical tool that enables interactive flow pattern recognition for the first time for general flow patterns has been presented. Furthermore, some new visualization approaches have been derived from these fundamental ideas. In this context, a special focus has been put onto the area of *comparative flow visualization*.

Bibliography

[AMP84] Yaser S. Abu-Mostafa and Demetri Psaltis. Recognitive aspects of moment invariants. *IEEE Transactions on Pattern Analysis and Machine Intelligence*, 6(6):698–706, November 1984.

[Asi93] D. Asimov. Notes on the topology of vector fields and flows. In *Visualization 93*, pages 1–23, San Jose, CA, 1993.

[BCH98] P. Billant, J.-M. Chomaz, and P. Huerre. Experimental study of vortex breakdown in swirling jets. *Journal of Fluid Mechanics*, 376:183–219, December 1998.

[BL90] P.W. Besslich and T. Lu. *Diskrete Orthogonaltransformationen. Algorithmen und Flußgraphen für die Signalverarbeitung*. Springer, Berlin, 1990.

[Bla85] Richard E. Blahut. *Fast Algorithms for Digital Signal Processing*. Addison-Wesley, January 1985.

[Bre65] Jack Bresenham. Algorithm for computer control of a digital plotter. *IBM Systems Journal*, 4(1):25–30, 1965.

[But03] J. C. Butcher. *Numerical Methods for Ordinary Differential Equations*. John Wiley & Sons, 2003.

[Can86] J. Canny. A computational approach to edge detection. In *IEEE Transactions on Pattern Analysis and Machine Intelligence*, volume 8, pages 184–203, 1986.

[CFS+06] S. P. Callahan, J. Freire, E. Santos, C. E. Scheidegger, C. T. Silva, and H. T. Vo. Vistrails: Visualization meets data management. In *ACM SIGMOD*, pages 745–747, 2006.

[Cli78] W.K. Clifford. Applications of grassmann's extensive algebra. *American Journal of Mathematics*, 1(4):350–358, 1878.

BIBLIOGRAPHY 149

[CLL92]   Pierre Comte, Marcel Lesieur, and Eric Lamballais. Large- and small-scale stirring of vorticity and a passive scalar in a 3-d temporal mixing layer. *Physics of Fluids A: Fluid Dynamics*, 4(12):2761–2778, 1992.

[CT65]   James W. Cooley and John W. Tukey. An algorithm for the machine calculation of complex Fourier series. *Mathematics of Computation*, 19(90):297–301, April 1965.

[DGH03]   Helmut Doleisch, Martin Gasser, and Helwig Hauser. Interactive feature specification for focus+context visualization of complex simulation data. In *VISSYM '03: Proceedings of the symposium on Data visualisation 2003*, pages 239–248, Aire-la-Ville, Switzerland, Switzerland, 2003. Eurographics Association.

[DH73]   Richard O. Duda and Peter E. Hart. *Pattern classification and scene analysis*. John Wiley and Sons, New York, Wiley, 1973.

[dLvL99] Wim de Leeuw and Robert van Liere. Collapsing flow topology using area metrics. In *VIS '99: Proceedings of the conference on Visualization '99*, pages 349–354, Los Alamitos, CA, USA, 1999. IEEE Computer Society Press.

[ES03]   J. Ebling and G. Scheuermann. Clifford convolution and pattern matching on vector fields. In Greg Turk, Jarke J. van Wijk, and Robert Moorhead, editors, *Proceedings of IEEE Visualization 2003*, pages 193–200, Los Alamitos, CA, USA, 2003. IEEE Computer Society Press.

[ES05a]   J. Ebling and G. Scheuermann. Clifford convolution and pattern matching on irregular grids. In *Scientific Visualization: The Visual Extraction of Knowledge from Data*. Springer-Verlag, 2005.

[ES05b]   J. Ebling and G. Scheuermann. Clifford Fourier transform on vector fields. *IEEE Trans. Vis. Comput. Graph.*, 11(4):469–479, 2005.

[ES06]   Julia Ebling and Gerik Scheuermann. Segmentation of flow fields using pattern matching. In Beatriz Sousa Santos, Thomas Ertl, and Kenneth I. Joy, editors, *EuroVis*, pages 147–154. Eurographics Association, 2006.

[FJ97]   Matteo Frigo and Steven G. Johnson. The fastest Fourier transform in the west. Technical Report MIT-LCS-TR-728, Massachusetts Institute of Technology, September 1997.

[FJ07]   Matteo Frigo and Steven G. Johnson. FFTW Home Page. http://www.fftw.org/, 2007.

[Flu00]   Jan Flusser. On the independence of rotation moment invariants. *Pattern Recognition*, 33(9):1405–1410, 2000.

[Fou03]   K. Fourmont. Non-equispaced fast Fourier transforms with applications to tomography. *Journal of Fourier Analysis and Applications*, 9:431–450, 2003.

[FP99]   Joel H. Ferziger and Milovan Perić. *Computational Methods for Fluid Dynamics*. Springer, 1999.

[Gar07]   Christoph Garth. *Visualization of Complex Three-Dimensional Flow Structures*. PhD thesis, TU Kaiserslautern, 2007.

[Hei00]   Stefan Heinrich. Skript zur Vorlesung Numerische Algorithmen, 2000.

[Her07]   Manuel Heringer. Entwicklung eines Mustererkennungsverfahrens zur merkmalsbasierten Visualisierung von Strömungsfeldern. Master's thesis, TU Kaiserslautern, 2007.

[HEWK03]   E. Heiberg, T. Ebbers, L. Wigström, and M. Karlsson. Three-dimensional flow characterization using vector pattern matching. *IEEE Trans. Vis. Comput. Graph.*, 9(3):313–319, 2003.

[HH89a]   J. Helman and L. Hesselink. Automated analysis of fluid flow topology. *Three-Dimensional Visualization and Display Technologies, SPIE Proceedings*, 1083(83):144–152, January 1989.

[HH89b]   James L. Helman and Lambertus Hesselink. Representation and display of vector field topology in fluid flow data sets. *Computer*, 22(8):27–36, 1989.

[HH90]   J. L. Helman and Lambertus Hesselink. Surface representations of two- and three-dimensional fluid flow topology. In *VIS '90: Proceedings of the 1st conference on Visualization '90*, pages 6–13, Los Alamitos, CA, USA, 1990. IEEE Computer Society Press.

[HH91]   James L. Helman and Lambertus Hesselink. Visualizing vector field topology in fluid flows. *IEEE Comput. Graph. Appl.*, 11(3):36–46, 1991.

[HJ04]   Charles D. Hansen and Chris Johnson, editors. *Visualization Handbook*. Academic Press, December 2004.

[HLD02]   Helwig Hauser, Robert S. Laramee, and Helmut Doleisch. State-of-the-art report 2002 in flow visualization. Technical report, VRVis Research Center, Vienna, Austria, January 2002.

[HS99]   D. Hestenes and G. Sobczyk. *Clifford Algebra to Geometric Calculus, A Unified Language for Mathematics and Physics.* Fundamental Theories of Physics. Kluwer Academic Publishers, Dordrecht, Boston, London, 1999.

[Hu62]   Ming-Kuei Hu. Visual pattern recognition by moment invariants. *IRE Transactions on Information Theory*, 8(2):179–187, February 1962.

[Jäh95] B. Jähne. *Digital image processing.* Springer-Verlag, Berlin, third edition, 1995.

[Jai89] A.K. Jain. *Fundamentals of digital image processing.* Prentice-Hall, Inc., Upper Saddle River, NJ, USA, 1989.

[JL97]   Bruno Jobard and Wilfrid Lefer. Creating evenly-spaced streamlines of arbitrary density. In W. Lefer and M. Grave, editors, *Visualization in Scientific Computing '97. Proceedings of the Eurographics Workshop in Boulogne-sur-Mer, France*, pages 43–56, Wien, New York, 1997. Springer Verlag.

[Jon98] David M. Jones. Acm computing classification system. Website, 1998. Available online at http://www.acm.org/class/1998; visited on July 14th 2008.

[KA05]   A. Koschan and M. Abidi. Detection and classification of edges in color images. *IEEE Signal Processing*, 22(1):64–73, January 2005.

[KCL00] Christopher A. Kennedy, Mark H. Carpenter, and R. Michael Lewis. Low-storage, explicit runge-kutta schemes for the compressible navier-stokes equations. *Appl. Numer. Math.*, 35(3):177–219, 2000.

[KHvdH99] L. H. Kellogg, B. H. Hager, and R. D. van der Hilst. Compositional stratification in the deep mantle. *Science*, 283:1881–1884, 1999.

[KK51]   J. F. Kenney and E. S. Keeping. *Mathematics of Statistics, Part 2, 2nd ed.* Van Nostrand, Princeton, NJ, 1951.

[Kol07a] W. Kollmann. Simulation of vorticity dominated flows using a hybrid approach: I formulation. *Computers & Fluids*, 36(10):1638–1647, 2007.

[Kol07b] W. Kollmann. Simulation of vorticity dominated flows using a hybrid approach: Ii numerical method. *Computers & Fluids*, 36(10):1648–1656, 2007.

[Kos95] A. Koschan. A comparative study on color edge detection, 1995.

[KP07]　　　Stefan Kunis and Daniel Potts. Stability results for scattered data interpolation by trigonometric polynomials. *SIAM J. Sci. Comput.*, 29(4):1403–1419, 2007.

[KWB+04]　Bill Kuo, Wei Wang, Cindy Bruyere, Tim Scheitlin, and Don Middleton. Hurricane isabel wrf model data. Available online at "http://www.vets.ucar.edu/vg/isabeldata/", June 2004.

[Lev92]　　Creon Levit. Visualizing the topology of vector fields - an annotated bibliography. Technical report, NASA Ames Research Center, 1992.

[Li97]　　　Yuguo Li. Wavenumber-extended high-order upwind-biased finite-difference schemes for convective scalar transport. *J. Comput. Phys.*, 133(2):235–255, 1997.

[Lig63]　　M.J. Lighthill. Attachment and separation in three-dimensional flow. *Laminar Boundary Layers*, 2(6):72–82, 1963.

[Lou01]　　P. Lounesto. Clifford algebras and spinors, second edition. Cambridge University Press, 2001.

[MAD05]　Abdelkrim Mebarki, Pierre Alliez, and Olivier Devillers. Farthest point seeding for efficient placement of streamlines. In Cláudio T. Silva, Eduard Gröller, and Holly Rushmeier, editors, *VIS '05: Proceedings IEEE Visualization '05*, pages 479–486, Los Alamitos, CA, USA, 2005. IEEE Computer Society Press.

[MH80]　　D. Marr and E. Hildreth. Theory of edge detection. *Proceedings of the Royal Society of London*, B207:187–217, 1980.

[MHHI98]　Xiaoyang Mao, Yuji Hatanaka, Hidenori Higashida, and Atsumi Imamiya. Image-guided streamline placement on curvilinear grid surfaces. In David Ebert, Holly Rushmeier, and Hans Hagen, editors, *VIS '98: Proceedings of the conference on Visualization '98*, pages 135–142, Los Alamitos, CA, USA, 1998. IEEE Computer Society Press.

[Mor07]　　Florian Morr. Vergleichende Visualisierung von Strömungsfeldern basierend auf Merkmalsextraktion. Master's thesis, TU Kaiserslautern, 2007.

[MP83]　　R. Machuca and K. Phillips. Applications of vector fields to image processing. *IEEE Trans. Pattern Anal. Machine Intell.*, 5(3):316–329, May 1983.

BIBLIOGRAPHY 153

[MTHG03] Oliver Mattausch, Thomas Theußl, Helwig Hauser, and Eduard Gröller. Strategies for interactive exploration of 3d flow using evenly-spaced illuminated streamlines. In *SCCG '03: Proceedings of the 19th spring conference on Computer graphics*, pages 213–222, New York, NY, USA, 2003. ACM Press.

[Oku70] A. Okubo. Horizontal dispersion of floatable particles in the vicinity of velocity singularities such as convergences. *Deep-Sea Res.*, 17:445, 1970.

[PJW06] Mark R. Petersen, Keith Julien, and Jeffrey B. Weiss. Vortex cores, strain cells, and filaments in quasigeostrophic turbulence. *Physics of Fluids*, 18(2):026601, 2006.

[Poi75] H. Poincaré. Sur les courbes d'efinies par une équation différentielle. *J. Math. 1*, pages pp. 167–244, J. Math. 2, 1876, pp. 151–217. J. Math. 7, 1881, pp. 375– 422. J. Math. 8, 1882, pp. 251–296., 1875.

[Poy03] Charles Poynton. *Digital Video and HDTV Algorithms and Interfaces*. Morgan Kaufmann Publishers Inc., San Francisco, CA, USA, 2003.

[PVH+02] F.H. Post, B. Vrolijk, H. Hauser, R.S. Laramee, and H. Doleisch. Feature extraction and visualization of flow fields. In *In Eurographics 2002 State of the Art Reports*, pages 69–100. The Eurographics Association, Saarbrücken, Germany, 2002.

[PW95] Hans-Georg Pagendarm and Birgit Walter. Competent, compact, comparative visualization of a vortical flow field. *IEEE Transactions on Visualization and Computer Graphics*, 1(2):142–150, 1995.

[Sch99] G. Scheuermann. Topological vector field visualization with Clifford algebra. Technical report, University of Kaiserslautern, 1999.

[Sch04] M. Schlemmer. Fourier transformation and filter design for Clifford convolution. Master's thesis, University of Kaiserslautern, 2004.

[SHH+07] Michael Schlemmer, Ingrid Hotz, Bernd Hamann, Florian Morr, and Hans Hagen. Priority Streamlines: A context-based Visualization of Flow Fields. In *Proceedings of the 9th Eurographics/IEEE VGTC Symposium on Visualization (EuroVis'07)*, Norrköping, Sweden, May 2007.

[SHM+07] Michael Schlemmer, Manuel Heringer, Florian Morr, Ingrid Hotz, Martin Hering-Bertram, Christoph Garth, Wolfgang Kollmann, Bernd Hamann, and Hans Hagen. Moment invariants for the analysis of 2d flow fields. *IEEE Transactions on Visualization and Computer Graphics (Proceedings IEEE Visualization 2007)*, 13(6):1743–1750, nov 2007.

[SHN+05] Michael Schlemmer, Ingrid Hotz, Vijay Natarajan, Bernd Hamann, and Hans Hagen. Fast clifford fourier transformation for unstructured vector field data. In *Proc. Intl. Conf. Numerical Grid Generation in Computational Field Simulations*, pages pp. 101–110, 2005.

[SJEG05] N. Svakhine, Y. Jang, D. S. Ebert, and K. P. Gaither. Illustration and Photography Inspired Visualization of Flows and Volumes. In *IEEE Visualization 2005*, 2005.

[SWH05] Jan Sahner, Tino Weinkauf, and Hans C. Hege. Galilean Invariant Extraction and Iconic Representation of Vortex Core Lines. In Ken Brodlie, David Duke, and Ken Joy, editors, *Data Visualization 2005: Proceedings of Eurographics/IEEE-VGTC Symposium on Visualization 2005 (EuroVis 2005)*. Eurographics Association, June 2005.

[SWHS97] Michael P. Salisbury, Michael T. Wong, John F. Hughes, and David H. Salesin. Orientable textures for image-based pen-and-ink illustration. *Computer Graphics*, 31(Annual Conference Series):401–406, 1997.

[TB96] Greg Turk and David Banks. Image-guided streamline placement. In *SIGGRAPH '96: Proceedings of the 23rd annual conference on Computer graphics and interactive techniques*, pages 453–460, New York, NY, USA, 1996. ACM Press.

[TSH00] Xavier Tricoche, Gerik Scheuermann, and Hans Hagen. A topology simplification method for 2d vector fields. In *VIS '00: Proceedings of the conference on Visualization '00*, pages 359–366, Los Alamitos, CA, USA, 2000. IEEE Computer Society Press.

[TWHS03] Holger Theisel, Tino Weinkauf, Hans-Christian Hege, and Hans-Peter Seidel. Saddle connectors - an approach to visualizing the topological skeleton of complex 3d vector fields. In *VIS '03: Proceedings of the 14th IEEE Visualization 2003 (VIS'03)*, page 30, Washington, DC, USA, 2003. IEEE Computer Society.

[VKP00] Vivek Verma, David Kao, and Alex Pang. A flow-guided streamline seeding strategy. In Tom Ertl, Bernd Hamann, and Amitabh Varshney, editors, *VIS '00: Proceedings of the conference on Visualization '00*, pages 163–170, Los Alamitos, CA, USA, 2000. IEEE Computer Society Press.

[VP04] Vivek Verma and Alex Pang. Comparative flow visualization. *IEEE Transactions on Visualization and Computer Graphics*, 10(6):609–624, 2004.

BIBLIOGRAPHY 155

[War97] Matthew O. Ward. Flow visualization. available online at http://web.cs.wpi.edu/ matt/courses/cs563/talks/flowvis/flowvis.html, February 1997.

[WE04] Daniel Weiskopf and Gordon Erlebacher. Flow visualization overview. In *in Handbook of Visualization*, 2004.

[Win04] Renate Winkler. Stochastic differential algebraic equations of index 1 and applications in circuit simulation. *J. Comput. Appl. Math.*, 163(2):435–463, 2004.

[YKP05] Xiaohong Ye, David Kao, and Alex Pang. Strategy for seeding 3d streamlines. In Cláudio T. Silva, Eduard Gröller, and Holly Rushmeier, editors, *VIS '00: Proceedings IEEE Visualization '05*, pages 471–478, Los Alamitos, CA, USA, 2005. IEEE Computer Society Press.

List of Figures

2.1	Generalized processing pipeline	10
2.2	Four comparative visualization methods	19
2.3	Illustration of the filtering process	23
3.1	Example vector patterns	45
3.2	Pattern recognition on the swirling jet simulation data set	46
3.3	Illustration of the pattern recognition process using Clifford FFT	50
4.1	Filter masks for Clifford color edge detection	59
4.2	Illustration of Clifford color edge detection	60
4.3	Constructed example, edge detection fails	62
4.4	Color edge detection applied to "cable car" image	63
4.5	Color edge detection applied to "Gaschurn" image	64
4.6	Color edge detection applied to "sports car" image	65
5.1	Difference between flow data and uncorrelated vector data	68
5.2	Different scaling possibilities for vector data	74
5.3	Graphical illustration of Lemma 5.1.2	84
5.4	Invariant moment values for prototypical flow features	90
5.5	Graphical representation of $\Psi_1 = c_{01}$	93
6.1	Moment masks represented as continuous 2D functions	97
6.2	Construction of a moment pyramid	99
6.3	Rotations in a Boussinesq flow	101
6.4	Swirling jet flow pattern recognition results	104

LIST OF FIGURES

6.5 Boussinesq flow pattern recognition results 106
6.6 Computation effort for the generation of moments and pattern recognition in the Boussinesq flow data set 107
7.1 Discrete streamline density definition 111
7.2 Flow diagram of priority streamline algorithm 113
7.3 Constructed Gauss-like filter for 2D-data 119
7.4 Filtering process illustrated in 1D 120
7.5 Priority streamlines for two dimensional artificial test data 122
7.6 Priority streamlines visualizing the swirling jet data set using varying settings 122
7.7 Priority streamlines visualizing artificial three dimensional data . . . 123
8.1 Comparative visualization of velocity (streamline density) and vorticity of swirling jet data 126
8.2 Convection in Earth mantle: comparative visualization using Priority streamlines 129
8.3 Comparative visualization of features in the mixing layer data using Priority streamlines 130
8.4 Screenshot of the *ComPARE* - visualization software 132
8.5 Interactive pattern recognition in multiple flow fields; pattern 1 . . . 133
8.6 Interactive pattern recognition in multiple flow fields; pattern 2 . . . 134
8.7 Interactive pattern recognition in multiple flow fields; pattern 3 . . . 135
8.8 Interactive pattern recognition for the first five hours of a flow simulation (Hurricane Isabel at 3150 meters height): three patterns are selected from a slice at an early time step. The patterns, which stay similar, can be tracked over time. 140
8.9 Moment pyramid (level one) comparison between the first and second time step of the Hurricane Isabel data (3150m height) for three different distance definitions. 141
8.10 Moment pyramid comparison with distance for two pyramid levels, different time steps 142
8.11 Moment pyramid comparison with distance between time step one and time step five for the first pyramid level (left) and the medium pyramid level (right). 143

Appendix A

Data Description

A.1 Boussinesq Flow

The Boussinesq flow was generated by a simulation implemented by Dr. Christoph Garth. The following data description is taken from our joint publication [SHM+07]:

"The data set is a classical Boussinesq approximation to simulate the flow generated by a heated cylinder. This approximation adds a source term proportional to the temperature (modeled as a diffusive material property) to the vertical component of the velocity field. The cylinder serves as a temperature source and thereby generates a plume of upward flowing material. As the plume moves upward, its outer layers exchange heat with the surrounding flow, resulting in inhomogeneous friction and hence turbulent flow."

A.2 Hurricane Isabel

The Weather Research and Forecasting (WRF) Model simulation data of Hurricane Isabel was kindly provided by Bill Kuo, Wei Wang, Cindy Bruyere, Tim Scheitlin, and Don Middleton of the U.S. National Center for Atmospheric Research (NCAR), and the U.S. National Science Foundation (NSF). The data, as well as a data description, is available online at [KWB+04].

A.3 Mantle Convection Data

The earth mantle convection data set was kindly made available by Prof. Dr. Louise Kellogg, Department of Geology, University of California, Davis, CA. The data indicates magma flow in the earth mantle. Further information on the data can be found at [KHvdH99].

A.4 Mixing Layer

The mixing layer data is a simulation generated and kindly made available by Prof. Dr. Pierre Comte, Institut de Mécanique des Fluides et des Solides, Univerity Louis Pasteur Strasbourg, France. More information about the generation of this data set can be found at [CLL92].

A.5 Swirling Jet Data

The swirling jet data was kindly made available by Prof. Dr. Wolfgang Kollmann, Department of Mechanical and Aeronautical Engineering, University of California, Davis, CA. The following data description is taken from our joint publication [SHM+07]:

"The development of a recirculation zone in a swirling flow is investigated by numerical simulation. This type of flow is relevant to several applications where residence time is important to enable mixing and chemical reactions.

The unsteady flow in a swirling jet is simulated with a hybrid spectral - finite difference method. The Navier-Stokes equations for an incompressible, Newtonian fluid are set up in cylindrical coordinates in terms of (complex-valued) streamfunction and pressure modes, which are governed by Helmholtz PDEs, and azimuthal velocity and vorticity modes, which are determined by evolution PDEs.

All equations are dimensionless containing the Reynolds number $Re \equiv \frac{v_z(0,z_0)D}{\nu}$ and the swirl number as defined by Billant et al. [BCH98]: $S \equiv \frac{2v_\theta(R/2,z_0)}{v_z(0,z_0)}$, where $z_0 = 0.4D$, $D = 2R$ is the nozzle diameter and ν the kinematic viscosity.

The PDEs for the Fourier modes are discretized in the meridional plane with 8th order central difference operators for the non-convective terms and with a 9th order, upwind-biased operator [Li97] for the convective terms. Time integration is accomplished with an explicit s-stage, state space Runge-Kutta method ([Win04], [KCL00]) where the Helmholtz PDEs for the streamfunction and pressure modes are solved at each stage, the present method is fourth order accurate with $s = 5$. The time step is controlled by the minimum of two criteria: The limit set by linearized stability analysis and the limit set by the error norms of an embedded third order Runge-Kutta *scheme [Win04].*

The Helmholtz PDEs for streamfunction and pressure modes are solved with an iterative method using deferred corrections and LU-decomposition of the coefficient matrices. The deferred corrections method is designed to reduce the bandwidth of the coefficient matrices. It converges rapidly using about ten to twenty steps, the rate of convergence increasing with the azimuthal wavenumber.

The simulation that was used for the current work results from the Reynolds number $Re = 900$ and the swirl number $S = 1.41$ within the range of the experiments of Billant et al. [BCH98] at a time ($t = 12.4$) when the recirculation bubble has formed and the initial symmetries of the flow field have been broken due to the disturbances introduced at the entrance boundary."

Further information on the data can be found in Prof. Kollmann's publications [Kol07a, Kol07b].

Selected Publications

Schlemmer, M., Hotz I., Hamann B., and Hagen, H.
Comparative Visualization of Two-Dimensional Flow Data Using Moment Invariants. Magnor, Rosenhahn, Theisel: Vision, Modeling, and Visualization (VMV'09), vol.1, pp. 255-264, 2009.

Meier, H., Schlemmer, M., Wagner, C., Kerren, A., Hagen, H., Kuhl, E., and Steinmann P.
Visualization of Particle Interactions in Granular Media. In: IEEE Transactions on Visualization and Computer Graphics, Vol. 14, No. 5, pp.1110-1125, September/October 2008.

Schlemmer, M., Heringer, M., Morr, F., Hotz, I., Hering-Bertram, M., Garth, C., Kollmann, W., Hamann, B., and Hagen, H.
Moment Invariants for the Analysis of 2D Flow Fields, IEEE Transactions on Visualization and Computer Graphics, vol. 13, no. 6, pp. 1743-1750, 2007.

Schlemmer, M., Hotz, I., Hamann, B., and Hagen, H.
Priority Streamlines: A context-based Visualization of Flow Fields. In Proceedings of the 9th Eurographics/IEEE VGTC Symposium on Visualization (EuroVis07), Norrköping, Sweden, May 2007.

Schlemmer, M., Hagen, H., Hotz, I., and Hamann, B.
Clifford Pattern Matching for Color Image Edge Detection - published in Hagen, Kerren, and Dannenmann (Eds.), Visualization of Large and Unstructured Data Sets, GI-Edition Lecture Notes in Informatics (LNI), Vol. S-4, 2006.

Hagen, H., Schneider, M., Schlemmer, M., Ruby, M., and Scheler, I.
Fast Voronoi Modeling - Computing, Special Issue on Geometric Modeling, Dagstuhl 2005.

Schlemmer, M., Hotz, I., Natarajan, V., Hamann, B., and Hagen, H.
Fourier transformation for unstructured vector field data. Proceedings of Ninth International Conference on Numerical Grid Generation International Society of Grid Generation, College of Engineering, San Jose State University, San Jose, California, pp. 101-110, 2005.

Ciolkowski, M., Schlemmer, M.
Experiences with a Case Study on Pair Programming, Workshop on Empirical Studies in Software Engineering, Rovaniemi, Finland, 2002.

Die VDM Verlagsservicegesellschaft sucht für wissenschaftliche Verlage abgeschlossene und herausragende

Dissertationen, Habilitationen, Diplomarbeiten, Master Theses, Magisterarbeiten usw.

für die kostenlose Publikation als Fachbuch.

Sie verfügen über eine Arbeit, die hohen inhaltlichen und formalen Ansprüchen genügt, und haben Interesse an einer honorarvergüteten Publikation?

Dann senden Sie bitte erste Informationen über sich und Ihre Arbeit per Email an *info@vdm-vsg.de*.

Sie erhalten kurzfristig unser Feedback!

VDM Verlagsservicegesellschaft mbH
Dudweiler Landstr. 99　　　　　　Telefon　+49 681 3720 174
D - 66123 Saarbrücken　　　　　　Fax　　　　+49 681 3720 1749
www.vdm-vsg.de

Die VDM Verlagsservicegesellschaft mbH vertritt

MIX
Papier aus verantwortungsvollen Quellen
Paper from responsible sources
FSC® C105338

Printed by Books on Demand GmbH, Norderstedt / Germany